M000316540

COURAGE TO LOSE SIGHT OF SHORE

HOW TO PARTNER WITH PRIVATE EQUITY TO GROW YOUR BUSINESS WITH CONFIDENCE

KELLEY W. POWELL

LIONCREST
PUBLISHING

COPYRIGHT © 2020 KELLEY W. POWELL
All rights reserved.

COURAGE TO LOSE SIGHT OF SHORE
*How to Partner with Private Equity to
Grow Your Business with Confidence*

ISBN   978-1-5445-1469-7 *Hardcover*
       978-1-5445-1467-3 *Paperback*
       978-1-5445-1468-0 *Ebook*
       978-1-5445-1639-4 *Audiobook*

To everyone who has inspired me to have courage.

*Those willing to be in the boat with me and those
who have trusted me to take the wheel.*

CONTENTS

INTRODUCTION

UNDER WAY, WINDWARD

I will never forget when I heard the news that would shape the development of my professional career.

I was at my desk at Royall & Company, where I was managing director for data, when I heard a commotion in the corridor just outside of my office. Our founder, Bill Royall, had passed on the highest bid. Our company, which provided student-recruitment support services for undergraduate colleges and universities, was being courted by several private equity firms. Eventually, an active bidding war ensued. But rather than going with the deal that would best line his own pockets, Bill had entrusted the company to the most qualified, right-fit partner to grow the business.

When he later looked all of his employees in the eyes and told us that these folks were going to support us as we grew in the right way—so we could do more for our clients, allowing us to deliver more value to them because of the resources and partners we would now have access to—we knew it was true. It was clear that what mattered to him was the long-term success of our clients, our employees, and the company. It was not about Bill. It was about all of us. And that made all of us want to stay and work even harder.

Our clients knew it too. We had always had excellent client retention, and that did not change. In fact, the process of the sale and the growth that followed resulted in so little disruption that many clients did not even know we had been bought. Royall & Company continued to put clients first and almost never took credit for our work—to the degree that, a few investment cycles later, when the company sold for $850 million and made splashy headlines in industry trades, there were companies up the street from us in Richmond that did not know who we were.

Having a front row seat for it all—seeing a founder approach private equity partnership in the right way and for the right reasons, and then implement that investment successfully—made me want to support every young founder who wants to do the same. After many more years at Royall & Company, I left with Bill's blessing to start my own company. As CEO of MacLaurin Group, I now lead my own business, which specializes in partnerships between private equity firms and the portfolio companies they acquire. But more on me later. Right now, I want to talk about you.

PUSHING BEYOND YOUR FEARS

I understand (and empathize with) the fears and challenges you are facing as a founder, or challenges you will face if you have plans to become a founder.

You realize you have taken, or soon will take, your company as far as you can. Growing your business, not to mention the process of finding a partner to support your growth, is scary. I get it. I see that reluctance in our clients all the time. And I have experienced it in myself. Talk to any successful leader, and they will say, "I'm scared every day." This is especially true for first-time founders.

Here are some of the fears I and my clients have faced. Do any of them sound familiar?

- *What you do not know.* You built the company on the skillsets of you and your co-founders, who may have also been your college roommates. That is not a bad thing; it is the embodiment of entrepreneurial spirit. Now you realize you have outgrown your collective skillsets. You don't even know how to begin having conversations about the appropriate way to grow, because you don't have experience doing things any other way.
- *The loss of control—but not of accountability.* You will no longer be in charge, and it is scary to give up control. You are accountable, after all, for your employees and clients. People are counting on you. How do you know you can trust a new partner? What if you choose an investor who does not share your values?
- *Airing dirty laundry.* Everything will be public. So far, when things are not pretty, you just deal with them and move on. You do what you need to do, because that is entrepreneurialism. But with an investor, all of your blemishes will be revealed—past and present.

- *The outsiders.* You know that growth will require an additional management team member, and you worry about a private equity firm assigning someone without your say. Your senior leadership team has a carefully curated culture, and someone who does not "get it" could muddy the water for you.
- *The vulnerability.* You no longer have the brazen confidence of someone with nothing to lose—because you have *a lot* to lose. What if you find a partner and try to grow your business, but it turns out this partner only wants your client list and mismanages it? Or, what if the plan for growth simply does not work? It would mean you are removed as CEO, or it may even be the death of your company—either way, your legacy ends.
- *Appearing needy.* Finally—and this is often unconscious—you may not be willing to admit that you have taken your company as far as you can on your own. It is natural to instinctively avoid that kind of self-assessment. It goes against who you are as a founder, to think that you cannot do it alone.

Any of these fears can keep founders from having the courage to risk growth. Uncertainty leaves us feeling too afraid to sail away from shore, much less to eventually lose sight of it. But no great voyage has ever consisted of merely hugging the coast.

So how do you build the courage to lose sight of shore? You find the right-fit partner for your business by taking time to anticipate what that team will look like, and by putting in the work to be a right-fit partner yourself. That is what you will learn in the pages that follow.

FAIR WINDS

Repeat after me: This process is not about money; it is all about finding the right fit for a safe journey and good fortune.

Okay, great, but how do you find fair winds to aid in your safe journey and good fortune? I have organized my advice—on how to navigate your journey from founder to partnering with private equity—into nine chronological steps, one per chapter.

Sticking with our sailing metaphor, here are the steps:

1. Demonstrate who you are as a person, so people will trust you as Captain. Private equity firms want to invest in leaders who do things the right way and who chose private equity with an understanding of what it means to take that investment. Tell your story through your actions.
2. Prove you can sail. Prove your company's value via the kind of clients it has attracted in the past and your ability to retain clients and revenue (and bring in new ones) even amidst rough seas.
3. Ascertain the seaworthiness of your boat. Know everything about your business before anyone asks, and make sure you can defend (or learn from) the decisions you have made in the past.
4. Determine what skills you and your crew lack, so you will know what you need in an Admiral. Do not just choose the highest bidder.
5. While seeking said Admiral, do not leave your boat unattended! Do not get so distracted by this process

that, at close, you no longer have a business to sell or cannot recognize your crew.

6. With your new Admiral, choose a route that your craft and newly expanded crew can handle. Have a long-term plan in place for growth that is challenging but clear for all to achieve.

7. Tend to the ship. Know when you need a bigger vessel and assess how to scale up, whether through technology or an add-on acquisition.

8. Go once more around the Cape. You are now in a cycle. This will not be a one-time event. What can you do with your collective wisdom now that you are all more experienced? Logistics will be easier as you now have your sea legs under you, but that does not mean the next voyage won't have rough seas, so prepare.

9. Rising Tides Lift All Boats. Invest in others, your community, and your passions, and you will continue to grow yourself and future leaders.

Partnering with private equity does not mean there will now be a "co-captain." There can ultimately only be one leader, one authority. Since private equity is buying your business, it is more akin to you as the Captain now having an Admiral. You are but one in the Admiral's fleet. You will still lead, but now you will also have a boss. This is why more than half of the book is dedicated to preparation, because if you do not choose the right Admiral—or you and your crew are unknowingly heading into stormy waters—there is little point in setting sail.

MY ROSE-COLORED SUNGLASSES

No matter what my role has been over the last twenty

years it has in some way, shape, or form, involved mergers & acquisitions.

The hard part in some of my past roles was watching from the sidelines as a merger & acquisition became more about the parts of a company than the founder and the people. Although that is a fine and worthy side of private equity endeavors, that is not the side I am interested in—especially after being on the management team at Royall & Company. I was able to see, firsthand, what can result when an investor is truly investing, so that the rising tide lifts all boats.

Ultimately, those experiences led to my interest in working with founders of small to midsize companies who want to continue growing their businesses, and with private equity firms who want to build instead of dismantle. So, in 2018, Jim Headley, Alan Williamson, and I co-founded the MacLaurin Group.

Even though we primarily focus on the technology aspects of sales and transitions, we also surround our partners with support for other parts of the process. Someone might initially seek us out because they have a technology question, but then we become an extension of their team in delivering on client success, thinking about return on investment, and—when speaking more specifically about private equity—the internal rate of return. The technology is there to support your business strategy, not drive it.

Sometimes we support private equity firms in their evaluations of potential acquisitions prior to a transaction. Sometimes we support private equity firms by advising their new portfolio companies during their transitions into a partnership. Sometimes founders come to us to evaluate them before a sale, before they even talk to an investment banker. Whatever the context, we basically work as an interim operating partner for founder-led companies undergoing investment. (In other words, you will not have to hire a Chief Technology Officer (CTO), Chief Information Officer (CIO), or Chief Operating Officer (COO) until the business is ready.)

The market we serve is very much about the founder, team, culture, and clients. It is *not* about dismantling, which is the key to our success.

In fact, I am so dedicated to paying it forward that we also invest in founders we believe in, literally. Are we a private equity firm? No. Typically, we do not even mention our portfolio-company investments as part of what we do. But it is very much a part of who we are.

Through our work, I have realized how opaque the process can seem from outside. Our founder clients say they wished they had known earlier how to better prepare themselves for future investment. Our private equity clients want us to support them in identifying the right deals, closing the deals in a highly competitive market, and quickly surrounding the portfolio companies with the support they need to grow from a good investment to a great investment.

So I decided to write a book. It is geared toward founders. By advising founders on how to better prepare, I also serve any private equity clients who may acquire these founders later.

A PASSION FOR PARTNERSHIP

I hope that while reading this book you will catch some of my passion for right-fit partnering, for finding those fair winds.

Although that passion has been formed by all my previous jobs and endeavors, it truly flourished during my time at Royall & Company. Royall was a Richmond unicorn: organic growth, homegrown, and with Bill staying involved through multiple rounds of investment. This book will include several sections about Bill and what I learned from him—first and foremost because it is excellent advice, and secondly to underscore my penchant for mentorship, both receiving it and giving it.

When I eventually left Royall & Company, it did not feel like I was stepping away from the executive team, but rather answering a call to give back and run towards what was next for me. It was a gut-wrenching decision. Instead of a resignation, I wrote Bill something more akin to a letter to a loved one, thanking him for the positive impact he had made in my life, both personally and professionally. I composed it while sitting in an airport in New York.

While writing and waiting for my flight, I could never have predicted what happened next. In a moment of pure serendipity, Bill walked out of the jet bridge at my gate. His flight had landed where mine was about to take off. He read my draft of a resignation there on the spot, gave me a hug, and said, "Thank you for all that you have done for our clients, our employees, and Royall. You need to do this. What can I do to support you?"

That was the moment I finally found the courage to sail away from shore and start a new business, knowing that all my mentors and collaborators will always be in the boat with me.

We even took a photo together. How many of us can say we have a photo from the moment we shared a resignation letter?

No one achieves anything alone. That truism should come as a big relief. No founder is expected to grow his or her company alone forever. True partnership is how we win the biggest of regattas, and within these pages I will show you how to launch *and* how to win. After all, the hardest part of any sailboat race is the start.

WHO YOU ARE AND WHO YOU ARE NOT

Enough about me, let's talk more about you.

This book is about a process. Certainly, not all founders stay. But if you are looking to make a fast exit, for whatever reason, this is not the book for you. On the other hand, if you are thinking about stepping away but care deeply about your employees, clients, and future growth of your business, then this book is for you.

If your business has been a $2 million company for the last ten years, and you are okay with that, this book is not for you. If you do not feel compelled to take it further—and that is fine—then you do not need a partner to help you grow.

If you want to grow and know just how to do it, but you

don't want a boss or to be bound to the advice and decisions of others, then private equity may not be for you. What you need is an assist: a little support. Knowledge can be bought by hiring the right advisor. Capital can be raised through a variety of means, including the classic bank loan. (The irony is that the private equity firm would have paid some of your asking price by raising debt on the strength of your company. But if you are in a good liquidity situation, then you may be able to raise significant funds on your own, although this comes with risk. Caution: Do not take on too much debt. That will not turn out great in an economic downturn.)

If following an honest look at your business, you realize it is a job and not a business, this book is not for you. In other words, if the business would disappear because you stepped away, like a sand castle washed away by changing tides, then you have made a successful career for yourself, but you do not have a business to sell.

If your company has no problems and is growing at a steady pace without aid, neither is this book for you. Either you do not need private equity investment, or you are only looking to cash out and sail into the sunset. To my colleagues and me, private equity partnership is not about the valuation or the raise. It is about what you do with the investment, and being accountable as an ambassador of the money to grow your business in a way that benefits your employees, clients, and investors. (Further, if you do think you want to sail into the sunset, you better be 100 percent certain. I have seen CEOs regret that decision after witnessing all the excitement and energy following a sale. They try to stay but only get in the way because they have already been replaced.)

Finally, this book is not a Rolodex of private equity firms, and it is not a formula for valuation or a guide to getting the most possible money. It is not a list of how to appear attractive but rather a guide for how to *be* attractive and how best to navigate the journey.

What I find most rewarding in right-fit partnership with private equity firms is getting to work with amazing founders who have incredible teams and inspiring business ideas, founders, and CEOs who want to keep growing in order to be of service to their clients and employees, and who are also humble enough to recognize they have taken it as far as they can. That is when true collaboration and real transparency will help you, together with your new partners, grow your business in a way you could never have been able to on your own.

You will have the support and structure around you to take care of your current clients while picking up new ones. And when it is done the right way, you will only need that support and structure for a short time. It is incredibly rewarding when I receive a phone call from one of our clients saying, "Thank you for setting our team up for success. I look forward to how we will work together again in the future." That means I have been effective in achieving the goals we set together so we can now move on, building on that accomplishment by supporting the next portfolio company.

My success is defined by your success. So let's make you successful!

WHAT IS PRIVATE EQUITY?

At a very high level, private equity (PE) is a form of investment fund that buys and sells private companies.

Here, I am going to dive into the characteristics of what makes private equity so unique and how you can leverage this world for your own company. While there are many different types of funds and investors, I will focus on the type typically involved with buying and selling founder-led companies.

Private equity revolves around the concept of a fund (the wind in your sails). A fund is basically a pool of money from a variety of different high net-worth individuals and institutions. The private equity company is there to raise and manage the fund, investing the money to buy companies, to make a profit and return that money back to the investors by selling the companies once they have grown. The fund can be any size, from ten million dollars to a few billion; that all depends on the private equity firm.

When a private equity firm first starts creating a fund, they will sit down and figure out the size of the fund they are looking to raise and the types of companies they wish to buy to be part of this fund. Now they must go and find people who are willing to invest in it, known as the limited partners. A common misconception is that there is a bank account with $200 million sitting in it, waiting to be drawn upon to buy companies. This is not how it works. When an investor commits say, $2 million to the fund (1 percent ownership of $200 million), they are obligated to make their percentage share available at the time of a transaction, not at the time of the fund raise.

Investors can come from high net-worth individuals, pension funds, university endowments, or family trusts. The one common thread that binds them is that they are looking to make a timely return on their money, within a period typically around three to ten years. Private equity thrives on repeat business, through trusted and known returns. The older and more experienced a private equity firm is, the easier (relatively) it becomes for them to find investors for their fund. This track record also serves as a metric for you as the seller of a company, so your new owners recognize the success you envision for your company. I will go over in later chapters how to evaluate the right-fit firm.

Once a fund has been raised (or the capital committed), the focus now moves to using the fund to purchase companies. We call the investors "limited partners" because they are limited in what they can do. All the trust is now placed in the hands of the partners of the private equity firm.

It is not uncommon for a private equity firm to have several funds active at the same time, each at different stages of their life cycle. Limited partners can be ex-founders or owners of companies that may have been purchased in a previous fund (and the good private equity firms will always look for these).

What makes private equity so attractive to investors is that, overall, it has a fixed return on investment. You are not betting on a single company or a given timeline. There is time and opportunity to make the necessary course corrections, or for a poor performing company not to pollute the overall profitability of the fund. The management of the fund is done in a way to minimize risk and give the private equity firm enough levers to maneuver changes in plans. This is why it is important for the fund to have a diverse set of companies, at different stages of maturity.

Private equity funds rarely go after pure startups; that is left to the venture funding of investment. These are seen as too risky for private equity. The ideal company for a private equity investment is one that has a strong customer base, consistent revenue, and good growth opportunities still to explore. I know companies that have been passed on, because they are number one in their space and have limited growth opportunity without a significant pivot. But a company that is maybe third or fourth in their sector is very attractive, as it shows there is a path for growth.

Typically, growth equity firms want the CEO to stay and still run the business because the equity firms have a minority interest. Buyout equity firms may want to replace you as a CEO and keep you around in more of a Chairman of the Board capacity rather than CEO. Even if a buyout firm says it wants you to stay, you will need to ask yourself if you will still want to work that hard the day after funds from the transaction are deposited into your bank account. Any private equity firm will be wondering and asking the same.

For a more detailed look into the investment types and returns, I refer you to the first few chapters of Adam Coffey's book *The Private Equity Playbook*, where he presents specific examples of the life cycle of a fund.

CHAPTER 1

WHO YOU ARE
AS A LEADER

Think about an Admiral considering leading a transatlantic voyage. Would he or she only inspect the boat they were adding to the fleet? Heck no. Far more important is the character of the person captaining the boat. Private equity firms—at least the kind you want as partners—do not solely invest in a product or technology, or even a roster of clients. They invest in leaders. They are not just thinking about getting in a boat. They are thinking about getting in a boat *with you*.

KNOW YOUR STORY

When I am deciding whether to invest in a founder, I want to know what that person's values and passions are, and how those values and passions shape the company. Further, I want to hear some biographical history and context: when, how, and why were those values and passions first forged? That context illustrates drive. In other words, I do not only want to know what you are committed to, but also why.

Now I understand you as a person. Now I believe in you. Now I want to invest in you.

However, because I am a technologist, when people meet with me, they usually do just the opposite. They try to sell me on their technology. More than once, our team has completely rewritten a company's technology in the span of a few months. And guess what? That is about how long private equity firms will spend considering you. So if your technology is the only value represented in your pitch, then your competitor could wipe you out before you even find an investor. The story of who you are as a person is an asset with much more longevity. And it can never be copied by a competitor.

Still, more often than not, when I sit with newer founders to start creating their pitch decks, they skip over themselves and jump right into the descriptions of their products and services. In my past, I have been guilty of this too. But from my experiences sitting on both sides of the table, I have learned that you must sell someone on who you are before you can sell them on what you do. Who you are determines what you do.

I had coffee once with a young founder, which led to a situation that perfectly illustrates my argument here. You will hear more about him and his business in a later chapter. For now I will say this: after our coffee meeting, I was positively jazzed. His is a business about relationships. His drive was authentic, personal, and meaningful. And he expressed a dedication to making the right choices for his clients, hiring and paying talented employees, and investing his own salary back into the business. What he needed from us was to advise him on technology. He reminded me of Bill, and he is the only founder I have ever asked Bill to meet and mentor.

But when he put together a sales deck and sent it to me, before the meeting with Bill, he had taken out his story. None of what he had told me over coffee was there. The second he changed the pitch deck to, "I am an online technology..." I thought, "Oh dear, not even I would want to write a check for this and I am already bought in." As soon as you are competing only on technology, you are no longer an indefatigable founder pushing forward for yourself and others. The magic is in the relationships.

He turned it around, of course, and now he has some kick-arse technology. I know because we helped him with his technology architecture, but I will never forget that moment. Know your story. Founders get starry eyed for buzzwords. I see it so much, I joke about it, "Oh yeah, I'm working on this data analytics platform that has AI to utilize blockchain with quantum computing for the zetta-byte era—and as long as I throw in enough buzzwords, you'll invest." Honestly, the opposite is true. When you do that, your pitch deck no longer has a focus or hook and suddenly begins to look like every other one I am reading. You become forgettable.

WHAT HAPPENS WHEN THERE IS NO STORY OR THE STORY IS NOT YOURS?

I recall a time we were involved in a due diligence on a smaller company with the interest of several private equity firms excited about their excellent, yet underdeveloped product offering. The only problem was that the employees came to work each day, did their jobs, and went home. There was no passion, no drive, no mission. They had a great product that was still doing what clients needed it to do, but the employees were on autopilot.

A son had inherited his father's company when he passed away. In the absence of a real successor to step in, the son took over for the sake of the employees and clients. His heart was not into leading the business. It was clear this was not the path for him. After some consultation with his accountant, he decided the best course was to sell the company while it still had some value.

But the company lacked a story. It did end up being bought, but not for as much as it might have if there had been a driving passion and vision behind it. Instead, it was absorbed into a much larger company. Fortunately, this gave the employees a renewed energy and desire to develop the product further. I share this anecdote for two reasons: first, to illustrate the power of story (or lack thereof), and second, as a reminder that people like to be part of something bigger. Your mission is not just a story but also a reason your employees will want to grow with you and deliver even better products and services.

WHAT HAPPENS WHEN THERE IS CONTRADICTION?

When your confidential information memorandum or pitch deck says one thing, but then I sit down with you in person, and what you say leads me to respond, "I am confused," or, "Maybe you can help me understand," I know in that moment we will not be the right fit for one another.

This came up in recent conversations with one of my colleagues, who describes his job as "a professional question asker." He told me, "Companies that are preparing for a sale always want to put their stories in the best light. And it is indeed up to the buyer to ask questions and take deeper dives to know if there are important details to understand that may have been omitted." Those details should not change the story.

Representing your company in the best light is very different from your story not ringing true. That puts everyone in an awkward position. Imagine for a moment you are sitting across the table from two equal partner co-founders who have successfully grown a business that generates multimillion dollars of revenue from software they developed while in school together and with minimal operating expenses. You are at the table because you believe in the founders and the mission.

Then you ask a few questions and find out there is not multimillion dollars in profit. Rather, their financials were not accounting for what would accurately describe the profit, which is closer to nonexistent. (Revenue is not profit. We will come back to that in the next chapter.) You find out the company does not own the IP for the software; rather, a separate consulting firm owns it. You ask a few more questions and learn there are not two founders but three. There really is not an equal partnership because it is clear in the conversation that one founder had the idea and the other founder had the ability to execute it. And the founder with the title of CEO has to apologize continuously for the miscommunications or misunderstandings (but never for the blatant misrepresentation of the truth). Would you continue the conversation? Would you invest?

You may be thinking, "That's just a hypothetical conversation."

I wish it were. That is a true story. The time I personally invested in learning about the company, and the time I took to sit across the table from them was a complete waste. I had been prepared to write a check. Like my colleague, I too, over the years, have become a professional question asker.

This is not to say the company will not eventually be hugely successful, but we clearly were not the right fit.

LIVE YOUR STORY

Your story is so much more than a piece of paper. It is who you are, how you live your life, and how you behave on a daily basis. The only way you will be able to sell your story is if it is true. And if your story is genuine and true, you do not turn it on and off depending on whether an employee, client, or investor is in the room. You sell it without even knowing you are selling. When you truly live your story through everyday actions, it becomes muscle memory.

It is rare for me to find myself in an airport, on a plane, or in a hotel elevator of a conference and not make a new introduction that will ultimately lead to a new business opportunity. It happens genuinely and authentically as I endeavor to be an ambassador for what I enjoy. It is all about engaging in conversation and listening.

Sometimes what is overheard can speak more loudly than what is communicated directly. I recall one particular flight while at Royall & Company, when I was traveling to Montana, to a university that had been a longtime client partner for us.

As I sat down for the last leg of the flight, prepackaged salad in hand, I made a brief and quiet call to tell my boys goodnight. I told them I missed them terribly and asked that they understand that it was important to Mom that I support our friends in Montana. I had a smile in my voice equal to the excitement for having this opportunity to be with and listen to our clients.

As I ended my call, the gentleman sitting next to me asked, almost apologetically, "If you don't mind me asking, what is it you do?" Naturally, before I answered his question, I introduced myself and asked the same of him. His reply was genuine, albeit not fully complete, "I am retired."

I began to tell the story of Royall & Company and answer his questions. Before I knew it, the flight had begun its descent, and my salad was still unopened. The gentleman handed me his business card, asked for mine, and asked for Bill to call him. He was retired, yes—as president of the university I was visiting but was coming out of retirement to support the strategic goals of another university. Now, he was hoping Royall would provide support to him.

I could not wait to send a note to Bill to share that he was right: Being an ambassador for Royall & Company had started the moment I stepped out of the office. He evangelized at every client pre-meeting that you begin a new journey the moment you head to the airport. The very best part of that particular trip happened well ahead of my intended agenda.

Your story is not what is written down in a presentation by someone who creates it for you. Your story for your company, your employees, your clients, and your investors is shown by your actions. Your story should not change when you are tired after three flights, or if your prepackaged salad remains unopened.

Those are the moments where your culture, passion, and excitement are shown through action. The clothes you wear while you travel, whether or not you take private conference calls in public places, how you treat service workers at the airport or the coffee shop—all of these things telegraph who you are as a leader and what it would mean to partner with you.

You are your story. The presentations you prepare for potential clients or investors simply echoes those actions, amplifying them over the water.

TELL YOUR STORY

Let's get into some more specifics about how to share your mission. Later in this chapter, I'll give you some questions to consider when you craft a pitch deck that includes your story. But first, make sure you have shared your mission and passion with absolutely everyone else connected to the company.

ONLY YOU CAN TELL YOUR STORY, SO WHAT DO YOU WANT TO SHARE WITH THE WORLD?

Most likely, you already know some version of your story in your head. Many of your clients and early investors probably do too. If you are a founder seeking private equity partnership, then you have already come a long way on your own, and much of that is a direct result of your values, mission, passions, and drive. Your only challenge now is to craft that story anew. The very best way to build that story is to start asking yourself some tough and revealing questions. Here is how to begin.

TEN QUESTIONS TO ASK YOURSELF

1. What was my passion for starting and growing my business?
2. How did I discover there was a need to fill?
3. Why was I uniquely qualified to start and build this company?
4. Who were the first people I chose to be in the boat with me?
5. Why did I choose that first client(s)?
6. Why did the client have faith in me and take a risk on me?
7. What has made the difference?/Why have clients chosen to stay with me?
8. What pivots have I made or what do I wish I had done differently?
9. How did I achieve a profitable revenue stream?
10. What do I need for continued growth?

A CASE STUDY IN EXCELLENCE

To illustrate just how powerful those ten questions can be, I will share Bill Royall's journey building Royall & Company as a case study. He started with a passion for direct marketing and created a business providing student and recruitment services for colleges and universities. In 2014, it was acquired for a valuation of $850 million. At the time, Royall & Company served about 290 universities and colleges as clients, and in the twelve-month period prior posted an estimated $109 million in revenue.

WHAT WAS HIS PASSION FOR STARTING AND GROWING HIS BUSINESS?

When Bill began Royall & Company in 1983, it was to support the growth of thriving businesses through strategic direct marketing (political campaigns and nonprofits). He was passionate about direct marketing because it is all about relationships and engaging people. Basically, he connected businesses with right-fit clients and connected customers with a service they needed. He was a matchmaker.

When he worked with a client in higher education, he found his noble mission. He wanted to reach students who had not considered an advanced degree to be something they could achieve, or who thought they would not find a university major that truly fit their skillsets and interests. And he wanted to reach students who never thought they could afford a college education, and connect them with scholarships. Doing so meant that he was also connecting schools with students with whom they could build long-term partnerships.

The satisfaction he found in serving colleges, universities, students, and families convinced Bill to shift the business focus to higher education in 1995.

HOW DID HE DISCOVER THERE WAS A NEED TO FILL?

Seeing the success Bill had achieved for business leaders, a trusted colleague asked him to apply his strategic direct marketing acumen to the recruitment of right-fit students to Hampden-Sydney College. That was in 1989. There were three colleges the next year, six colleges the following year, and then twelve colleges the year after that. In 1995, when Bill made the decision to grow a direct-marketing company focused on higher education, he was already serving twenty-six colleges in support of their strategic missions.

WHY WAS HE UNIQUELY QUALIFIED TO START AND BUILD THIS COMPANY?

As an entrepreneur, Bill was expertly experienced at supporting other visionaries who wanted to grow their businesses. He had a special skill for building relationships and engaging people. He proved again and again how to engage audiences in ways that made those audiences want to learn more.

WHO WERE THE FIRST PEOPLE HE CHOSE TO BE IN THE BOAT WITH HIM?

When Bill first started, he was alone. But he knew eventually he would be surrounded by incredibly talented individuals who would represent something greater than just Bill. So he added the "and Company." Ultimately, the "and Company" was a fundamental component of his success, as well as a part of his values, which he cultivated in others.

You could probably guess the first people in the boat with him: a client ambassador to take client calls and office support for accounting and billing. He invested in account managers, program managers, and technology to ensure Royall & Company delivered on its promises. Bill expected himself and everyone he hired to commit themselves to serving others. Because he focused on culture, he also hired someone to recruit and retain those who believed in the mission.

WHY DID HE CHOOSE THAT FIRST CLIENT?

Bill chose to invest his time in advising a trusted colleague. He listened. He genuinely wanted to support. The relationship was already there.

WHY DID THE CLIENT HAVE FAITH IN HIM AND TAKE A RISK WITH HIM?

The client took a chance on Bill because of his track record delivering on his promises. He had already proven his success as a direct marketer. There was no other business offering similar to direct marketing for colleges and universities.

WHAT MADE THE DIFFERENCE? WHY DID CLIENTS CHOOSE TO REMAIN CLIENTS YEAR AFTER YEAR?

Clients made the decision to stay with Royall & Company because Bill held the entire team accountable for delivering on promises year after year. Bill was listening to the data and what that meant for a client's return on investments even before business analytics were cool. Bill understood that you repeat what works well.

Every client he served was his most important client. Bill expected everyone to always take a phone call, no matter what they were doing—and that meant even during a meeting with Bill. We had intercoms everywhere to hear pages from reception when a client would call. And when I say everywhere, I truly mean everywhere.

WHAT PIVOTS DID HE MAKE OR WHAT DID HE WISH HE HAD DONE DIFFERENTLY?

The pivot was when he leaned into higher education. As for his 20/20 hindsight, I once heard him tell a young founder he wished he had taken more time with family and friends, because as an entrepreneur the business can consume you. (I will tell this story later.)

HOW DID HE ACHIEVE A PROFITABLE REVENUE STREAM?

Bill had a passion for anticipating and ultimately delivering services that would improve the lives of students and their families. He took seriously the responsibility to protect the reputation of every client and the institution of higher education. The return on investment from engaging the services of Royall & Company resulted in a multiple return for those institutions. The success was created in partnership, through customer service, and by being available when clients needed him.

WHAT DID HE NEED FOR CONTINUED GROWTH?

Bill surrounded himself with a mission-driven leadership team and private equity partners who had the experience to support scaling up, while continuing to hold everyone to the same high level of customer service, which always included delivering on promises.

BUILD A COHESIVE CREW

Once you have your story, tell it to every employee, mentor, advisor, and early investor. Anyone who might one day represent your company needs to be aligned with your mission and values.

Let's return to our boat analogy: a private equity firm will be getting in your boat, not only with you, but also with everyone else you have already invited onboard. You need to be thinking from day one about who you bring on your team, especially at the management level. Although everyone will be different and bring their own skills and value to the crew, they still need to be aligned with your mission and values. And that will be easier to do when you have defined these from day one, because you will be assessing fit based on the mission and values. You will need to remind and reinforce those continuously.

I sat down with a startup founder recently who was advertising for a position in his C-Suite, but he neglected to articulate anything in the job description about who he is or what the company is all about. He had only detailed the technology requirements. I said, "So just to be clear, you are recruiting for someone who needs a job and has a skill?"

You should want more than that. You want this hire to be on the journey with you. You want to make sure that they care about growing this company and can become a trusted advisor and member of your crew. Then you can say, "Oh, by the way, we also need you to have this technological skillset." This may seem obvious, but I am telling you that some of the most important moments of your story are sometimes the easiest to take for granted. Your story as a founder will also be shaped by how you recruit and retain the right people to join your team, full stop.

"It's all about finding great people with whom you share a chemistry," Bill said, while I spoke with him about writing this book. You have to be able to excite one another and instill in one another a passion for the work. Then he added, "Values need to be aligned. And, it is also important to remember values must be cultivated—that requires leadership."

Bill did this by holding company town halls, meeting with employees one-on-one, and embracing a team approach when meeting with clients. The result is that employees were constantly reminded of Royall & Company's mission. We wanted the work we did to be good for colleges as well as for families and students. So Bill hired management team members who lived the culture and values every day, and applied those to the business by relying on each of our individual talents and looking through each of our personal lenses. Understanding that leadership is taught by example, Bill not only did this himself, but also expected each person on his management team to reinforce the company's mission by setting that example.

Rob Healy, of L Squared Capital, was a partner with Chicago Growth Partners when it purchased Royall & Company in 2007. He also spoke to me for this book:

> "The ability not only to hire top talent but also to retain them speaks to leadership," he says. "It's not just that people are joining a team to be paid the highest dollar. Rather, they join a team because they are needed, will be empowered with responsibility, and will be allowed to run their aspects of the business to see the fruits of their labor. Leaders who prioritize correctly will continue to be able to do this for their employees even under the pressure of high growth. This is the kind of team you want to have in place already. After my first meetings with Royall & Company, I knew they not only took care of their clients but also each other. Every employee was loyal and committed, and believed in the mission."

Private equity firms want to invest in leaders who have a foundational mission and the ability to align all of their employees around it. Know what your story is because you will definitely be asked. Companies are a dime a dozen, but true leaders are priceless. Find out what drives you and sell that.

CLOSING THOUGHTS

We've talked a lot about storytelling and for good reason. It is the most effective sales tool you have. Once you know your story—and are living it—heed this last piece of advice.

While writing this book, I was fortunate to speak with Adam Coffey, three-time CEO, currently of CoolSys, and author of *The Private Equity Playbook*, an excellent guide to private equity partnership. (I knew he and I would be simpatico before we even spoke, not least of which because we have both worked on executive teams for Tom Formolo, who has since started New Harbor Capital.) In my conversation with Coffey, he noted the importance of making sure you and your team are the ones telling your story. "Oftentimes, the management team doesn't bring the story, so the investment bankers have to," he says. "And then buyers doubt the story because the management team isn't selling it."

Never expect anyone else to translate your passion for you.

Further, he explains, if the story doesn't feel authentic to you and your team, you won't be able to sell it effectively. "If you're saying you can achieve four times return on capital, do you actually believe it yourself?" You better.

Now that you can prove your integrity, it is time to prove your skills.

MYTHS OF PRIVATE EQUITY

If you mention private equity to the average person, it may carry a negative connotation and be seen as the industry that destroys companies in search of the almighty profit, irrespective of who gets in the way.

This "greed is good" attitude has been built up over the years through various media stories and movie portrayals where private equity has swept in to feed on a company's assets. In these instances, private equity companies are portrayed as vultures devoid of human compassion or true vision. Our archetype is Edward Lewis, played by Richard Gere in *Pretty Woman*, who makes a living breaking up companies, along with his slimy lawyer who enjoys the process a little too much: "Morse's jugular is exposed. It's time for the kill. Let's finish this. Call the bank." No wonder private equity has such a bad reputation. (Though most people do not remember the end, in which Julia Roberts's character, Vivian, shows Edward there is another way, that growing and building something with the company could be far more fulfilling. This miraculous change of heart is perceived as the exception not the rule.)

When you think about it, the myth of asset stripping or breaking up companies to sell off is not a sustainable model by any stretch. It does not make sense. You cannot keep taking something whole, split it up, and expect to reap a greater value. Yes, there are times where this approach is needed—and I appreciate those who help companies navigate it—but as the old saying goes, "[a company] is greater than the sum of all its parts."

While you explore this new world of private equity, allow me to dispel some of the myths that may be circulating.

They break up companies. As I have already touched upon, this is probably the biggest myth. Conversely, private equity spend a lot more time acquiring and merging companies than breaking them up, through what is known as tuck-in acquisitions, where a smaller company is absorbed into a bigger one to round out a feature set or open up a new market area.

In the rare times where a company does need to split, it is more likely than not a division that is no longer core to the mission of the company and is sold off to continue to have a life elsewhere. One example of this is Microsoft selling off Expedia in 1999. The travel site enjoyed a $10 billion revenue in 2017.

They do not care about the people. Private equity would be nothing without the crew that runs it. The only real currency that private equity deals in is human capital. They need the right people in the right roles doing the right job to create growth and wealth. Private equity cannot afford to indiscriminately fire people; there would be no one left to run the company. They like to keep the expertise that has built up over the years with the company.

Yes, they will bring in additional talent to advise on any knowledge gaps. I will go into more detail in later chapters why this is a huge benefit, as their network of experts go deep and wide into areas in which most company owners simply do not have access.

When creating the deal structure, it will be the private equity firm that will be looking to create a share pool to incentivize employees and key managers, and I have personally witnessed instances where this pool is larger than the founder may have even previously considered.

They are only interested in making money for their partners. This one is partially true. The myth implies that it is only the direct partners in the private equity firm that are making the money. In reality, the firm is interested in creating returns and wealth for their limited partners, the ones who wrote the check for the fund. These limited partners are our pensions, university endowments, mutual funds, and other various financial vehicles to which our money is put to work. In other words, these partners want you to succeed.

They will instruct an arrogant youngster to tell me how to run my business. This is one I hear a lot and it usually comes down to a miscommunication. A private equity firm has a number of people associated with it who will support the partnership going forward. They range from the most senior partners, to principals, to associates, who although often young, are among the most committed and hardworking people you could hope to meet. These are your crew, there to support you in making the right decisions and executing your plans.

The best associates, with whom I have worked, will never tell you what to do but be there to support your communication with the senior partners. The advice I give to new founders and CEOs in the private equity space is to treat associates like trusted members of your team, not as your new boss. Anything they give you is a suggestion or hint, at best, not a directive. Directives will come directly from partners—and do not worry, they will not hide behind associates.

I will lose all control. Will you lose all control? No. Will you lose some control? Yes. Of course you will, and if you think otherwise then private equity may not be for you. But the control you lose pales in comparison to the opportunity and experience you will gain.

Private equity will never come in and tell you how to service your customers; that is your trade, your knowledge, and expertise. Where a private equity firm will provide value is in your strategic thinking. They will encourage you to think bigger or wider, and then give assistance in execution. I keep talking about the partnership that is crucial to a successful private equity engagement, because if truly embraced through that lens, then everyone strides forward and continues to grow. Bringing private equity into your company is accepting assistance to get you somewhere that you may have struggled to reach alone.

There are bad actors in all industries and life. Private equity is no different. Not everyone is good. A good myth is steeped in some form of truth, but more likely than not, it is seen from a single point of view, where the context of that event is not truly articulated. Private equity is where the vast majority of our money (pensions, mutual funds, etc.) is put to work to create wealth for all those involved in the system, from the jobs being created at the portfolios, to the founders and shareholders when a transaction occurs, to the banks (and their shareholders) that lend the debt to finance, to the limited partners that ultimately celebrate their benefits at the end. In fact, there is a whole ecosystem of beneficiaries. The rising tide truly lifts all boats.

CHAPTER 2

WILL IT FLOAT?

Now that you have proven your value as a Captain, you will need to make sure potential Admirals know you have a sturdy and seaworthy craft. You can give tours of your boat, discuss the materials used to build it, show off the blueprints, and let them examine the mast, boom, sails, hull, and sheets (for the inexperienced sailor, ropes on a boat are called sheets), but they still do not know for sure that it will float. The only way to demonstrate that is to put it in the water and sail.

Similarly, the only way to prove your business is valuable—that it fills a niche, provides top service, and is strong enough to handle recessions and threats—is through your client longevity and your survival history. Let's talk about clients first.

CHOOSE THE RIGHT CLIENTS, AND BE SURE THEY ARE PROFITABLE

There is no better indicator of a good investment than when a company's first clients are still around. When a private equity firm sees that you have high client retention, it sees recurring revenue. It sees lifetime value in your clients. Happy clients suggest that your company is poised for long-term, exponential growth. It is not about turning over old clients to get new ones. What really excites investors is when you can say, "Yes, I am confident we will attract many clients next year, in pace with our growth—*and* that is above and beyond the revenue stream we already have, because we will retain our current clients. And, with your investment, I will soon have the bandwidth and infrastructure to support further growth."

Your happy lifetime clients will be your references for potential investors when you are on the market. We will talk about how to use them as references, as well as how to keep clients happy (and grow with them) before you go on the market. But first, know that none of this is possible if you are not getting the right clients from the very beginning.

Sometimes when founders are starting out, they just want to bring in any revenue they can find. But if the clients you are taking on are not connected to the core focus of your business, then you are in the wrong business. Either that, or the revenue you are bringing in is coming at the cost of distraction. You should either be in that other business, or turn down the revenue from poor-fit clients.

Otherwise, you are wasting your time, especially in the long term, because in order to grow with those poor-fit clients and continue to meet their needs, you will have to veer away from the core focus of your business. The alternative would be to eventually lose those clients, and then you have an unfortunate track record of losing clients. This is why it is paramount to get the right clients from the very start.

Do not be distracted by just any revenue. I had a roll-on-the-floor-laughing moment when Bill recalled a time when he was first starting out. He was presented with an opportunity to market video cameras. He bid on the proposal and won it. He did not "know a damn thing about marketing video cameras." He admits looking back that it was not a smart move. He brought in revenue with the project, but it was a total diversion. The fast money, even at the beginning, was not worth pulling him away from building the business he wanted to grow.

Sometimes the distraction is client relationships that are no longer the right fit. I remember a time Bill told a client they had become "a dumpster fire." What? It's true. He remembered too. We were in the Rosser Reeves conference room. It was the end of a very long meeting where it was clear the client was having internal struggles, political battles, and turf wars, and was simply not displaying their ability to interact even within their own team. Until they could get their internal interactions in a better place, they had little chance successfully engaging with an outside partner.

It seems like a very simple thing to do—cut your losses with clients when they are no longer a right-fit. Sometimes it is the best decision you can make for the success of both parties, but there is always a tug on the loyalty heartstrings when that happens. No leader wants to make the decision to let a client go. In an honest self-assessment, I have struggled with that decision more than once myself. It is a hard thing to say to a client, "This is no longer a mutually beneficial relationship," but it is sometimes necessary for everyone's benefit. One of two things will happen when you have that conversation. The best outcome is that you adjust the relationship and get back on track for a right-fit partnership. An equally good outcome is you free yourself from a distraction to your business, and the client finds their right-fit partner. You are then able to focus energy on your right-fit clients and mutually beneficial relationships.

Nasser Chanda, CEO of Paymerang, a client of MacLaurin Group, made the decision to step away from one of his largest clients soon after taking on his role as CEO. There was, for good reason, concern, pushback, and questions why he would make a decision that would seemingly have a negative impact on revenue. Chanda is a seasoned CEO. He has been down the path of "those damn video cameras" himself and learned from it. Although it was not the most popular choice to step away, Chanda did. He explained, "Strategy is all about making choices, and before you decide what you want to do, you have to decide what you don't want to do. We all have limited time and resources." Turns out Chanda made the right decision (we will hear more from him in later chapters).

So who is your "right" client? The one who needs what you are selling and is willing to pay a fair price for it.

PROFITABLE CLIENTS ARE THE ONLY CLIENTS

The other thing I hear from a lot of young entrepreneurs is, "Yeah, my business has x number of clients, but we are not yet bringing in any revenue." That is when I challenge them, "Well, no, you do not have a business. You have a hobby...or community service at best." Who is not going to allow you to do something for them for free if it benefits them?

Let's say you have developed a mobile app where students sign up for free to share their experiences about colleges and universities, under the agreement that you will not share or monetize their data. If in your pitch deck your business model revolves around monetization of this data in some way, you have an immediate problem—this is not your data to sell.

The biggest problem that you have is that the perceived value of your business is predicated on a falsehood. The data you have cannot be monetized, and as soon as you change your terms and conditions, that may have an impact on the quality or quantity of data being collected.

As an investor, it makes no difference to me if you have one student using the system or a million. The value is still the same: zero.

Not only are you not bringing in enough money to pay the bills but, further, you have no way of knowing whether or not what you are selling has any value. And if you do not know that, then a potential investor will not either.

Getting the right client and setting the right expectations from the start is key for successful growth.

If you are reading this and you have not yet started your

own company, you are probably thinking, *"This sounds obvious."* But when you are a founder, and you have put your own money—and possibly your friends' and family's money—on the line, you are terrified of failing. Having an unhappy client leave because they did not get what they paid for sounds a lot like failure. Novice founders will do anything they can to minimize the risk for potential clients, including offering services for free.

Further, frankly, a lot of founders are not "traditional" salespeople. They are good at selling their vision and why they are creating the company. But that does not mean they are good at pipeline, cold calling, and following up. If you are not comfortable telling potential clients that you need them to pay you, then find an advisor or someone on your team who can. You must be certain you are delivering value in a way that people are willing to pay.

That is not to say that your first clients should not have the benefit of an agreed-upon beta discount or initial-partner discount. Or maybe you let them delay their payment by tying it to a deliverable, taking the risk out of it for them. Bill told every client, "If you don't think that we have delivered on our value to you, don't pay us." In the more than twenty-five years, I know of only one client who ever took him up on that.

It is a big mistake, however, to think that you can eventually prove you have a market just by taking on nonpaying clients. All you will prove is that people like free stuff. A market is a collection of people who have a need great enough to compel them to pay you. Full stop.

And if your first client is not paying, imagine what happens when the next round of clients you are approaching call that first one for a reference.

"Oh, I highly recommend this product."

"Great! How much did you pay for it?"

"Well, I didn't."

"Even better—I'll get it for free too."

Instead, you want them to say, "I paid for this product, I highly recommend it, and I am renewing because I see value in staying with this company." That is true buy-in and partnership. Remember the point in the last chapter about revenue not being the same as profit? Private equity will not only care about revenue, they will also care about your profitable customers. It is important for a company to know which customers are profitable and also why they are profitable. The process of servicing a profitable customer must be repeatable. Do you know which of your clients are the most profitable? Do you know why? It might surprise you to learn it is not always your highest paying clients who generate the highest revenue.

GET IN FRONT OF THE RIGHT PEOPLE

So how do you find these clients? Ideally, you already know them.

The most successful founders are the ones who were in the trenches of their industry before, which is exactly how they discovered the gap they are now filling. Being so close to it, they obviously identified people with that need. Then, during market research, they identified more people who needed what they will be selling. When I started MacLaurin Group, I was already having conversations six months before launch. We had existing clients before day one.

And, of course, it is always better to have a connection introduce you to the clients you seek. I think we can agree you cannot just stand on the street corner somewhere, holding up a sign reading, "I hope you'll be my first customer." There is a lot of trust that goes into being someone's first client. That is why, back to the pricing conversation, it is perfectly fine to offer pricing aligned with the goals you and your first clients want to achieve together. You are saying, "I want you to help me vet what this product should or should not be. In so doing, you are partnering with me on that." They are essentially helping you develop and prove an idea. But it is still your idea. You are bringing it to them. So they should not have an expectation to get it for free.

Also, (and again, this seems obvious) you cannot waste time focusing on clients that do not need exactly what you are selling. Look for the most appreciative customer; that is the customer who provides the highest opportunity for growing successfully together, with the lowest risk, and where all your needs align. For Royall & Company, that was undergraduate enrollment. And when someone told Bill he should reach out to for-profit schools as well, he chose not to. He knew those schools had a completely different formula for success and that he could not just apply the model of his product to them. (I will discuss this more in chapter 4.)

As a founder, you must have the courage not to pitch the wrong revenue streams. People will ask you to do a lot of things, and you need to know where your model is replicable and where it is not. And remember, any investor will evaluate your clients and ask if those clients represent the type of newer clients they wish to attract.

Your first clients need to be as vested as you are in the success of the company. There is no better way to get someone vested than to: 1) solve a problem and make their life easier; and 2) provide them with a concrete way to determine the return on the investment of their time and money into your business. If they are putting in zero dollars, they will never see your partnership as more than a value of zero.

KEEP YOUR CLIENTS HAPPY

Private equity firms will want to understand not only the clients you have now and in the pipeline, but also the clients you lost. Be prepared for them to ask why those clients left. It will be important to understand what went wrong, and if there is a risk of the same thing happening to current clients. So I want to spend some time discussing how to keep clients.

The importance of your first clients is not about their name recognition for your brand. They are not a badge to use in marketing. Instead, they are your best asset as you grow and develop your product. Since they are on the front line of using your product, they will know what works and what can be improved. They will also hear from your competitors and can alert you to who is coming after your business.

You may think you know what your clients want, but your clients *really* know what they want. Getting a product right takes a lot of time. Getting a product perfect can take a lifetime.

As Joan Isaac Mohr, one of Royall & Company's first clients said, when I called her while working on this book, "Your first clients know your faults, warts and all, so if they stay with you, they will be the most loyal clients you will ever have."

Those loyal clients will forgive rather than jump ship. You want someone who will grab an oar, not pull the plug. They can also promote you to prospective clients and convince your newer clients to "hang in there." They will support your reputation.

To keep these clients, you must nurture them. Keep them close. And then ask them to help identify the direction and growth opportunities they see for your future. You cannot pay for that kind of service—because there is literally not one available.

How this manifests itself can come in many forms.

This is your first lesson with early clients: the "go light" for a reference referral does not stay on forever.

A reference is not a broad brush of permission to use them when you wish. Like a personal reference, you should always treat it as merely an opening to invite them if they wish to participate at the time. This is even more true when it comes to business references, where reputation and brand is important to protect.

I recall a time I advised a young founder who was responding to an RFP (Request for Proposal). As part of that process, the founder needed to provide three reference clients. He was excited, as he had permission for references he could easily use and was keen to move forward with the document.

You must be absolutely, 100 percent sure you have permission.

You must check. And while you are checking, if they are okay with you being a reference, it gives you a wonderful opportunity to check in and make sure everything is going as well as you think it is.

In the instance of the young founder I was advising, when he did call all three of his references, he received the green light from all but one. What? This was a huge blow and took the wind out of our young founder's sail. What to do next? Being a seasoned sailor on these seas, I had quite the opposite reaction. I recognized this as a huge gift that had just been delivered to us.

Yes, there were problems with this client that should not have remained unresolved for so long. This client should have been contacted long before now, and the problem remedied. Do not assume silence from a client to mean all is well. The good news is that the client was supportive. They did not wish to say anything to others that may harm the founder or the business. The client was asking the founder to help them reframe their current truth by fixing the problems before they were called for a reference. After all, remember that clients want you to be successful to help them be successful. They want to support and help you get it right.

After addressing the problem head on, taking the time to figure out what the issue was and resolving it, the problematic reference turned out to be his strongest, noting "Well, it hasn't always been perfect, but when it wasn't, he cared enough to check in and fix the problems."

If I were on this reference call as an investor, I would be most interested in hearing that a founder put in the effort to check in and make things right with a client. That is who I want to be in business with.

Your clients are not only income. They will be your word-of-mouth advertisers and your references.

CHECK IN AUTHENTICALLY

You will want to check in with your clients from time to time, of course. But you should never do so simply by asking, "What's going on?" How do you check in with clients authentically? Well, that is complicated. You have to make sure you understand their business. It is hard to check in if you do not understand your client's demands. Always have a specific reason to call. Keep track of the last time you were in touch with each client and the reason for the conversation.

When I asked Bill to discuss the best practices for checking in on clients, he boiled it down to: "It's important to be in the moment with them rather than be a distraction."

In other words, your approach should be different for every

client. Clients should not hear from you only when they are receiving an invoice. They should hear from you when you need nothing from them, when you are calling just to listen. A lot of companies believe they have amazing customer service, but they do not. It is something you have to be very deliberate about.

Making sure you are not an interruption means calling clients to check in when you know they might truly need your support. An example of this is when I reach out to a client as they are preparing for a board meeting, to ask if there is anything we can do to support them in advance of it. We know roughly when their board meetings are, so we can schedule our connections at the times they are most useful.

HOW TO EXECUTE ON AUTHENTICITY

Checking in with clients can be simple. Here are a few hints:

- Set up a Google alert for every single client. Whenever they are in the news—if they hired a new executive, or are about to expand into a new office building—reach out to say congratulations without them having to tell you what has happened. In the case of an expansion, do not become an interruption by adding on to a heavy workload. Allow more time to pass before going beyond your congratulations. When it will not be an interruption, you can ask, "What are the goals? What strategy do you have ahead of you, and are there ways we can be supportive?"
- The best service you can provide to your clients is

knowing what keeps them up at night. That happens from understanding where they are. You cannot just pick up the phone and say, "I know nothing new about you. I am wondering if you could tell me something new about you." When you are in conversation with your clients, you must truly listen. Ultimately, it comes down to empathy: understanding when it is convenient or inconvenient for you to call, knowing what they are or are not facing at any given time, and then reserving your thoughts and input on how best to offer support until after you have truly listened to them.

- Maintain regular checkpoints along the way, in which you request feedback about your products and services (ideally immediately after whichever part of the engagement is related to your question). Even then, lead with appreciation.

- Devote moments for appreciation that are not immediately followed with an ask. I know this sounds like basic etiquette, but you would be surprised how frequently people call to say, "Hey, I just wanted to thank you—and while I have you on the phone, let me ask you this favor..." The best way to show appreciation is when you expect nothing in return. Otherwise it will feel like manipulation and not appreciation. Keep it to "thank you"—just "thank you." And don't do it at the end of the day, when your clients are working to meet a deadline.

HOW NOT TO DO IT

We have all been at the wrong end of an inquiry call. If you do any sort of press release, you know you are inviting the worst business development "professionals" to insert themselves into your daily routine.

This game is known only too well by most private equity firms after closing a deal and announcing it. A wave of emails soon come flooding in, expressing faux excitement and false praise as a way to pitch services. Jim Milbery, of ParkerGale Capital, who spoke to me for the book, sums it nicely: "It starts with a single sentence fragment: 'Dear Jim, Congratulations on closing [Company Name]...' and it turns into a pitch for their services."

It is not about the portfolio. It is an interruption and a huge distraction.

It shows a lack of understanding in the massive undertaking that is in closing a deal at a private equity firm. "It's generally all-hands-on-deck across the firm," Milbery says. "When a private equity firm gets a deal closed, the whole team is exhausted, and often they are catching up on other portfolio work that piled up over the last week of the closing process—sifting through reams of emails and returning phone calls. The last thing we want is to hear pitches from service providers, chock-full of what is thought by them to be fancy buzzwords, which only further illustrate the fact that they know very little about the company."

Put yourself in the client's seat. Be in the moment with the client rather than a distraction. Do some basic research by reading their website and news releases, and knowing their marketplace. Know the cadence of their industry. Know when is a good time to make that call and, more importantly, when it is not a good time.

I have it on good authority that if you get it wrong, some

private equity firms will put your whole domain on the blacklist of their incoming email server. Not kidding.

HERE IS WHAT IT LOOKS LIKE IN ACTION

I am sure you have heard the school myth that the person in charge has all the answers. They must show strength and never let slip any weakness or doubt. We all know this is nonsense but yet, when we find ourselves in a position of leadership, we hold onto that old stereotype and before we know it, we have shut down all avenues of constructive feedback.

We have to be willing to accept the things that we do not want to hear and resist the urge to blame the messenger. We have to listen and act upon it accordingly. That might be an employee looking to make things better or a client describing an issue. They may have a point or they may not, but always assume their intentions are good and have the courage to listen. This will most likely take you out of your comfort zone.

Clients are the strongest set of people you have in the boat with you. Their success relies on you being successful enough to deliver the service or product they require from you. So not listening to them is irresponsible at best and hubris at worse.

Creating a successful client is not the same as client success. When I asked Tom Willoughby, Vice Chancellor at the University of Denver, to share lessons from Bill's leadership, he said, "My advice to young founders is to be a servant leader who is passionate about the success of your clients."

If you take the time to genuinely care about your clients, they will care about you. If you take the time to listen to your clients, they can help you more than you may first appreciate. If you authentically respect your clients, they will tell others about you. Or as Mohr illustrates beautifully, "Make them a star and they will include you as a star in their galaxy."

In who's galaxy does your star shine?

TRANSPARENCY AND TRUST

What should be consistent among all of your client interactions is the goal: to have client relationships defined by transparency and trust. In later chapters, I will discuss how to approach trust and transparency with your clients during a transaction. Before then, you need to have built the foundation.

At the heart of any meaningful engagement is trust. To show trust, honesty, and authenticity, we must be willing to allow ourselves to be vulnerable.

Trust is earned by creating an environment where it can flourish. To create an open environment means it must also be a safe place where the group commits to one another the permission to be completely open and honest. Even better is an environment where all can learn while having a bit of fun.

This is something you simply cannot will into existence. You cannot simply say, "This is a trusting environment," and suddenly everyone embraces the idea. You have to lead by example. Show your trust and vulnerability. Trust is a unique emotion: the more you show it, the stronger it grows.

If you do not build trust with your clients, they will never give you honest feedback, and without that, you are sunk. A company that has atrophied instead of adapting to its market is not attractive to investors. You want to be able to show that you are not only open to feedback, but that you welcome it and seek it without ego or fear, because you know that it is the only way to improve.

Show that their courage to bring the matter to your attention was well placed and you have taken it on board. Now you have created a bond that will only grow stronger, and you as a leader will benefit from it. As Tom Willoughby explains, he took a chance on Royall & Company not only because of Bill's knowledge, passion, and track record, but also "Because of his interest. Bill was more interested in learning about me and the institution I represented than telling me about himself and his company. That impressed me."

Trust does not mean you have to have all the answers all the time. When one of my now partners was first introduced to me through private equity, I do not think he was fond of my penchant for what I call "the 'no update' update." Early on in a project, I scheduled a weekly update meeting to discuss progress. He responded, "Feels like a waste of time as I know now that I will have nothing to update you on in a week's time." I said that was okay and set up the meeting anyway.

But even he eventually came to appreciate "the 'no update'

update" as a positive way for us all to keep on top of our individual contributions. Silence can be detrimental to internal communication and trust building. Eventually, when colleagues passed me in the office, instead of saying "Hello" or "Good morning," they said, "Still no update" followed by a grin. I didn't mind this good-natured joke, because I was now receiving near real-time updates unsolicited!

It is the same with clients. Building trust means sometimes you must be comfortable with sharing "the 'no update' update." Especially during what a client considers a crisis. Clients will have patience, trust, and understanding when they know you are working on their behalf. Do not leave them wondering if silence means you have forgotten them. Commit to a time to call and honor it even if you only have a "'no update' update." Hold yourself accountable not only for scheduling those calls, but also honoring them. Clients should not wonder when they will hear back, nor should they have to call to check back in with you. Chances are your "'no update' update" can at least tell them what you have ruled out as potential causes of crisis. Providing a confirmation of no update is in fact an update.

WEATHER THE STORM

Just as we want a well-built ship that will weather the storm and keep us safe, private equity prefers companies that will weather their storms, or in financial terms, an economic recession. (We all have definitions of what a recession is, but if we look to the National Bureau of Economic Research, it is defined as a significant decline lasting more than a few months, and being visible in "real

GDP, real income, employment, industrial production, and wholesale-retail sales." This can happen at a national level, but also more locally at a company level.)

Recessions are a fact of life and cyclical in nature, even though they are hard to predict. But come they will. The issue that you must address is how you will handle it when it does come. This is what every business needs to do. When you are entering the private equity world they will wish to see, demonstrably, how you are going to cope when the recession cycles back in again. The best indicator of future resilience is to look at the performance of your organization in the last recession, what lessons were learned, and what processes were put in place.

In a typical recession, overall spending is reduced with nonessential or luxury items usually being cut in the consumer space. The problem a recession can bring to light that can long outlast the downturn term is that the customer has an opportunity to see what life would be like without said product or service. The customer may decide it was never mission critical in the first place and, therefore, will not reengage in better times.

Some companies are considered recession-proof, as they provide the very things we all need no matter what is happening, such as food and service companies. (We still must eat and have things repaired.) Some companies can even thrive in a recession, as their product is designed to reduce costs or make things more efficient. Then we have the companies that are not really geared up for a prolonged period of downturn, and may have to lay off staff, or in the worst case, close their doors completely.

It is important to determine with which one of the three types your company more closely aligns and show how you have coped historically when the economy is heading towards a downturn. Private equity firms are looking for the pitch-deck slides that illustrate how the company has weathered that period historically. Even companies that are typically recession proof can find themselves suddenly at risk of bankruptcy during times of a health crisis.

If you as a founder suddenly find yourself in an economic downturn, you have an opportunity to prove your company is resilient, or you are resilient because you can pivot. This is important because on the other side of an economic downturn, private equity is going to be searching for founders like you.

Howard Marks, the co-chairman and co-founder of Oaktree Capital Management and author of *The Most Important Thing: Uncommon Sense for the Thoughtful Investor* offers advice to readers to avoid being a forced buyer or forced seller, writing, "being a forced seller is the worst. That means it's essential to arrange your affairs so you'll be able to hold on—and not sell—at the worst of times. This requires both long-term capital and strong psychological resources."

LOCAL STORMS

There are other storms that a company must weather that are a little closer to home. It is good business sense to get ahead of each and formulate a plan. As you seek private equity investments, it is important to be thoughtful about how you will weather these storms before talking to the private equity community.

One storm that can be hard to predict is the one of a shifting market. What happens when your product or service is no longer fashionable or even required? Think Blockbuster missing out on buying Netflix and completely underestimating the magnitude of streaming content, which resulted in the disappearance of the home video market. Or Kodak, the once-photography company that sniffed at digital photos and did not really prepare itself for the ultimate Trojan horse of smartphone cameras paired with the internet. If the big boys can miss a market change, then what makes your company immune?

Maybe you have had to pivot already and can show you have evolved with the changing voyage. This is something that will excite a private equity firm, to see the map of how you are getting ahead of the next evolution. If your company relies on a very specific condition that exists in the marketplace, then you must be prepared to answer the question, "What if that condition is no longer valid?"

Another area that is becoming increasingly risky is one of exposure. We are in a time where extraordinarily large companies dominate. Think of the reach of Amazon, Google, Microsoft, or Apple, to name a few. These are household names that have legions of loyal customer bases. Your product may manage to sail without one of these huge barges sensing the disturbance of your wake. You may be filling a gap they are missing and have been missing for many years. However, what happens if they blink and spot your space in the market and decide to close it? This happens more often than not, and I have seen many a company become completely irrelevant overnight because

AWS or Google decided to offer your service for free as part of a natural product release.

I have witnessed private equity companies perform their market research within due diligence and conclude that the company is sailing too close to big barges and the risk of being run over, literally overnight, is too great to proceed. The management has no real answer to the threat, and until the company innovates itself out of it, they will find themselves under water.

MORE WAVES

The waves created by customers, and to a degree suppliers, can also threaten damage to your vessel. This is an area of risk I see sinking many a good deal before it even leaves port. If your company is too reliant for a large portion of its revenue to a handful of customers, this will make private equity nervous. If those clients were to go elsewhere, how does that impact your bottom line? A strong distribution with no reliance on a single customer is ideal.

And now, let's discuss your suppliers.

I have seen where a great company has built up a wonderful recurring revenue from a large, strong user base, yet the whole thing is predicated on the fact that they are the exclusive licensee for a given resource. The license that is not perpetual but agreed upon each year from the supplier. It has been renewed for the last twenty years, so there is no reason to think it will not be renewed going forward, right? But what if that supplier decides not to renew, or offers it to another? Then the company would be in serious trouble.

Private equity cannot trade on goodwill. They need more certainties than you may be able to provide.

The private equity company that is potentially partnering with you will most likely be looking to sell you again three to five years out. They will try to model as closely as possible what your company will be like, so they can determine potential future value to the next buyer. They need your company to grow—to go after new markets, new clients, new products. They cannot enter a shrinking or extremely narrow market. They want to know and understand all the risks as much as possible before entering into a commitment. This is not the time to bury your head in the sand and take the "we will cross that bridge when we get to it" attitude.

It is important to ask yourself the tough what-if questions when it comes to your survival. You are the best person to answer those and give yourself an honest evaluation of just what are the big waves that could take down your ship. There are areas that may already keep you up at night, but you exude the confidence to your team and employees that they need not worry about such an outcome. A good solid plan for growing your clients will give everyone the confidence that the ship you steer can weather whatever storm or waves are thrown at it.

CLOSING THOUGHTS

You have clients who are paying for your services, are happy, and will make excellent references. You have the ability to prove that you would not be a risky investment because you have weathered storms in the past. Congratulations, you have all of the skills needed to sail! Great, that means it is time to assess your boat.

HOW DO PRIVATE EQUITY FIRMS MAKE THEIR MONEY?

A private equity firm is a company too. They have the same wants and desires any company has—to grow and be profitable. They have expenses like any other company, office space, employees, stationary. But where does their revenue come from?

The purpose of a private equity firm is to manage a fund, from raising it to buying companies, to managing the companies through to selling them. For this they charge a small yearly management fee to the limited partners. This is around 2 percent of the invested amount. That is not a huge amount and not enough to make the fortunes of anyone working at a private equity firm. In some instances, a private equity firm may charge the portfolio a monthly or quarterly management fee.

The bulk of their money will come from the time of a sale when the profits are realized. A private equity firm will take a percentage (around 20 percent) of the profit from a sale as their revenue, returning the rest of the profit to the limited partners.

For a well-performing company, they may look to return the investment early through special distributions, so they can effectively play with free money—a technique used by successful day traders too, incidentally.

Alan Williamson, CTO of MacLaurin Group, will always use a poker analogy to describe this. He is a far better poker player than I am, so for this let's use his analogy. Imagine sitting down at a poker table with $100 provided by your limited partners. You play strategically, thoughtfully, and after a few wins, you are sitting with $200 at the table. Instead of risking the full $200, you take $100 off the table, and give that back to your limited partners. You are now left with $100 of "free" money, to which the limited partners can still lay claim. You have moved the risk of their investment to zero, while still allowing them to enjoy a significant upside when you eventually step away from the table.

Let me break the poker analogy here quickly, because a private equity firm never takes risks or bets. Everything they do is calculated, to minimize risk, and show a return to their limited partners.

It is for this reason that private equity can be so attractive for investors. With the right choice of companies inside of a fund, the limited partner may never be called upon for more than 40 to 60 percent of their committed capital. Think about that. You commit to $2 million but only $800 thousand may, in fact, be invested to realize the value of the full amount. This allows the investor to make their money work double for them.

Understanding this positions you to think in the same mindset of the average private equity partner and how they think of how to make money. To make their money and to make money for their limited partners, the company must be successful, and ultimately sell.

What does this mean for you as someone entering the private equity space?

It means you are entering a cycle, a process that turns every three to ten years. The private equity firm that you just sold to will eventually look to sell you. They have to sell. It will not be anything personal, and it should not come as a surprise. It is the natural order of things.

This is not a bad thing, and as I will explain in chapter 8, this cycle can be broken if the buyer is not a private equity firm. This can happen if the buyer is a strategic buyer (someone looking to you as their add-on acquisition), a merger (when two companies are aligned enough, coming together makes sense), or a management buyout (taking the company back to private again).

Hopefully as each evolution of the cycle happens, you are becoming wiser (and all being equal, wealthier) and know what makes a successful private equity partner for you as you look to the next few years of growth under new ownership. Your role is to ensure continuity to the rest of the business so such events are really non-events to your employees and customers. I will go into this in more detail in chapter 8.

CHAPTER 3

BAD NEWS, PLEASE

If you were only selling your boat, perhaps you would not care to investigate its weaknesses. You would not need to be cognizant of necessary repairs or areas that could be enhanced because Buyer Beware, right? If they do not know that mismatched paint is an indication of prior accidents, or that discolored upholstery suggests a leaky port, that is on them.

But you are not selling your boat. You are trying to convince an Admiral to join you in the boat and then take off on a new journey together. If you do not know everything about your vessel, why would anyone risk journeying with you? And if you are not completely forthright about all of your vessel's weaknesses, why would anyone trust you enough to even climb aboard?

When seeking private equity partnership, there is absolutely nothing to be gained from hiding blemishes. Even if you do hoodwink an investor—and I guarantee you will not—our navigation map would be based on faulty information, meaning you would not meet your growth goals.

Rather, embrace your mistakes and receive feedback as a most precious gift. Remember that anecdote in the last chapter about the founder who asked three clients to be references for an RFP? Ironically, it was the unhappy client that wound up being the best reference. Investors heard that the founder had provided excellent customer service by fixing a problem. Great. Even more important is what investors were able to surmise: that this founder knows how to stumble and get back up.

I want to partner with someone who knows how to fail. People who have never had to struggle scare me a little bit. My reaction is, "Oh dear, what is going to happen when we do fail?" I want to know that when something is less than perfect, you will have a calm, helpful, and proactive response. I need to know how you function under fire. And if you present your company as if it is all roses, that makes me skeptical.

Everything that has ever gone wrong in the history of your company provided you with an opportunity to fix a problem and then (humbly) brag about it later. And you find these problems/opportunities by seeking feedback. That is why I call it a gift—the gift that keeps on giving.

This chapter is dedicated to the due diligence process and the importance of running toward feedback. As you have surely gathered by now, I do not mince words. I do not want to waste your time. Clients choose to partner with me because they know I will speak candidly and openly in service of collective success.

Feedback is not personal. The only personal part is that

the person giving it is invested enough in your success to be honest. And when that advice is coming from a trusted, expert advisor, it is an even bigger gift. That expert is expensive, and they are not going to spend the hour of time you have together complimenting the things they discovered are going well. In other words, feedback conversations are negative by nature. That is what you want. Sometimes founders have to change the narrative in their heads a little bit before they enter the due diligence process. If you are going to be overly sensitive or not want to hear the things we have to say, then you are going to continue to see people walk away.

I say this so much in my family that it has become a joke, a term of endearment, among my children. One of them will criticize me and the other will say, "Feedback is a gift, Mom. Run toward it!" and I have to laugh because it is true that we need those around us to hold us accountable.

Further, you must constantly seek feedback. It will not just come to you. As a founder, you should be doing some kind of small checkup every year. And you can definitely turn to your clients for help. Again, as we discussed in the previous chapter, do not burden them when it is a disruption. But when you have their ear, make a humble and candid request, "What can we do better?" Sending a survey will provide insight, but it does not replace or garner the same meaningful quality of response as a direct question.

When you can demonstrate a history of seeking feedback and responding to it by implementing change, you will be more valuable to investors down the road, both because your company is stronger, and because you have demonstrated a dedication to the process.

But that's the general advice. Let's get into specifics. Later I will discuss the process of undergoing a due diligence led by a private equity firm. First, I want to stress the importance of conducting a reverse due diligence—meaning you hire an outside firm to evaluate you *for* you—first.

USE BINOCULARS

As a Captain, you want to be the first to know what is ahead. A quality set of binoculars will bring into focus distant sights. Similarly, you want to anticipate what a firm will later learn about your business during the due diligence process.

I cannot emphasize this enough: conduct a reverse due diligence before you even put your company on the market.

First of all, any private equity firm interested in you is going to hire someone to execute a due diligence for them anyway. A buyer will never know your business like you do. Therefore, it does not matter how well you pitch your life's work—they will always look to a third party for independent evaluation. Whatever is going to come up *will* come up. So why be surprised in the moment, when you have a limited amount of time to address it?

Doing your own reverse due diligence gives you power and information. Not knowing what issues might impact your sale will not only affect the number of potential buyers you have, but also the type of buyer you will attract. Obviously, it will also affect your cost. And since you will likely have to delay after the issues come to light, it affects your timeline too, which could ultimately endanger the closing of a deal. Besides, you do not ever want a potential buyer to be the one pointing out your own company's problems!

When everyone knows the company's needs, you will all be better able to recognize right-fit partners. You already know there is something you need supported, or why would you be seeking partnership? The more you understand what it is you cannot do on your own, the better able you will be to pick a partner. No one is expecting your company to be perfect, so lead with your problems. Private equity firms want to hear about what you cannot do, and find out if it is something they can do for you.

Private equity investors are not afraid of getting their hands dirty, but they need to know how to support you. What you might consider a "weak marketing team," they would consider an area for growth and therefore return on investment. And maybe marketing is their specialty. Your weaknesses may be why they want you. If they believe in you as a founder, and they think you have incredible employees and clients, and the few things you have not been able to do on your own are exactly the sort of things they can do, then you find your boat "under a red sky at night, a sailor's delight," as the saying goes, and there will be smooth sailing ahead.

Author and CoolSys CEO, Adam Coffey, points out that doing your own research in advance allows you to shape the story, giving you more control over your company's narrative as you go on the market. "Pay advisors to do a market study," he says. "Perform the quality-of-earnings for yourself. Don't wait for a potential buyer to ask you for it or hire advisors to do it."

Use the information you glean from the reverse due diligence to assess potential buyers. How do they respond to it? What can they offer specifically related to it? Coffey says, "Don't just look at the money private equity brings to the table. Money is not operators. You want operators to help you."

Some of you may be thinking, *My right-fit partner will find me regardless of whether due diligence happens before or after we start talking.* Maybe. But what about the firms who are not even close to being your right-fit partner? If you wait to let them find out after executing their own due diligence, you have just wasted everyone's time. Five years later, when you are up for sale again, guess who will remember that you wasted their time?

WHAT IS A REVERSE DUE DILIGENCE?

I want to leave the sailing analogy to the side for a moment because whenever I advise clients about the due diligence process, I use a different and very effective comparison: the home inspection. Assume you are selling your family house in a traditional real estate deal. You know there are rooms in need of a coat of paint, but overall, it is in good shape. You kept up with repairs and nothing major has gone wrong in a long while. You are sure others will fall in love with the house as much as you have. This will be the easiest sale in real estate history.

Then that first home inspection report comes through from a potential buyer and it is littered with problems. Now you are in defensive mode, trying to put a value on each item in order to see the transaction through.

Would it not have been nice to see that home inspection report before the buyer did—before you even attract potential buyers? The only way is to pay to have your home inspected yourself. Historically this has been seen as unnecessary, but nowadays realtors frequently recommend the practice because what the $400 report yields is invaluable. Not only does it ensure you correct issues and therefore put a better product on the market, which will yield a better price, but it connects you with home buyers who want what you are selling. There is never a claim of "bait and switch." You control the narrative. No one wastes anyone's time.

A similar process happens when someone considers purchasing your company. This, as I'm sure you know, is called due diligence. A team of experts investigates one or more areas of your company, creating an assessment for the private equity firm to think about during its decision. This report highlights strengths, weaknesses, and areas of concern.

Of course, selling a company is far more complicated than selling a house. Getting as much detail as possible about the state of your asset is invaluable before buyers start poking around. What you can fix will make you more valuable. What you can't fix will change how you position yourself. This is why investment bankers increasingly advise performing a "mock" or "reverse" due diligence prior to sale. Unlike with buyers on the housing market, if the sale of your business falls through, you will likely not have several more people coming to tour next week. Instead, you will have to take your asset off the market and strategize another attempt down the road.

CONSIDER YOURSELF A TECH COMPANY

The key to success is engaging a professional due diligence firm, an outside third party that will go through the process as if they were doing it on behalf of a buyer. Except for this phase, you will want this process to go deeper and wider than a typical inspection. You will receive a true, unbiased view of your organization and how it stacks up against similar types of companies your size in your industry.

Although an accounting firm will most likely be able to perform a good analysis on your financial health and processes, accounting firms are typically less likely to assess your technology, an often overlooked area of business. This is why you want to bring in external parties who specialize in technology assessments. Is this exactly what we do at the MacLaurin Group? Yes. Am I trying to sell you our services? No. I don't care who you call. Just call someone. The reason I'm even in this business is because I am passionate about the need we address.

And if you don't think you are a tech company, you are likely underestimating the contribution that data and technology contribute to your bottom line. Even Bill would have described Royall & Company as a marketing company in the early days, although in reality, he had a data-driven marketing company.

Is your IT team involved in more than just providing desktop and back-office support? Do you have a monthly datacenter or cloud bill? Do you have any custom software that powers either an internal or external process? Do you have one or more databases that hold data unique to your company? Have you engaged an external development company to support you? Would your service or product suffer dramatically if any of your IT systems (outside of email/finance) went offline for a few days? If you answered yes to even one of these questions, you have technology that private equity firms will want to assess to make sure it can support the growth and expansion they have in mind for your business.

Sadly, in my experience, business owners often overlook the importance of assessing their tech. In particular, non-tech founders typically lack the necessary skills to truly understand whether or not their IT departments are doing what they should be doing, or even if the person they hired is capable of the job. Things may appear to be fine, but like watching a duck swimming on the water, you as the founder probably do not have a real understanding of how frantically feet are paddling under the surface. Ask your technology leader if he or she fears what is still left undone before setting sail for the growth ahead.

Too many times, I see deals damaged or destroyed by a lack of knowledge and leadership in this area. Examples include founders who did not know their systems lacked security, or that their platforms were functioning on severely outdated technology or, in extreme cases, that their contracts were not properly administered, and ownership of the platform is not even theirs to sell. This is why it is imperative to execute your technical due diligence early. I have seen private equity clients wait—they want to check every other box in the deal process first—and then deeply regret that decision. When things go wrong, the cost of walking away from the deal will be far greater than the price tag of an early tech due diligence.

TAKE THE OPPORTUNITY TO PRACTICE

Another reason to hire a third-party professional due diligence firm: the process will be as real as possible, giving you and your team the opportunity to practice. The process should feel like a conversation, not an investigation. Getting your team ready means ensuring they feel confident and open enough to answer questions honestly, while at the same time managing the level of detail that is shared. A good due diligence firm will provide feedback and train your team on how best to present your company.

Again, this is especially important for your tech teams. Not all technologists are experienced as "client facing" and may be uncomfortable participating in the process. If you are worried about them being interviewed, let them practice.

WHAT TO DO WITH THE INTEL

Of course, the most important reason to perform the reverse due diligence is to gain insight into the current state of your business. Some problems you will want to fix immediately. Others you will at least be aware of. A private equity firm never wants to see something come out in due diligence that catches you off guard. You do not either, because then they wonder whether or not they are willing to take on that extra load and for what price.

FIX WHAT COULD CAPSIZE YOUR CRAFT

First and foremost, you want a reverse due diligence to discover any potential deal breakers. For example, are your finances above board? It cannot just be that you, the founder, have been doing your books. You need to make sure you have an accountant who has shored them up. Investors do not want to wade into messy waters like that.

A less obvious problem that comes up often during my work involves the ownership of intellectual property rights. Especially in technology, founders sometimes contract consultants to advise them. If they failed to be explicit with the contract when they had a product built out, there is a chance they do not fully own the intellectual property (commonly referred to as simply "IP"). Some firms might say, "Okay, we can work through it. And we will have to before the transaction." Maybe they have expertise in the area. You will be delayed, and it will all cost more money, which neither party will prefer, but for whatever reason they are willing to move forward—great.

Many firms, however, will say, "Forget it. It is not worth it. We are walking away." But when you figure this out in advance, you can either fix the problem, or allow firms to self-select based on their willingness to fix the problem.

When MacLaurin Group performs a due diligence on a portfolio company, we also walk the founder through the results. These are the areas you want a potential partner to be an expert in, these are the things you need to fix before putting yourself in a sales process, and these are the things you need to fix whether or not you go on the market. And yes, most importantly even if you say you have something in place, such as security, embrace a partner like us who is going to trust *and* verify.

No one wants to buy a company with an open security vulnerability—but they might be interested in how you handle your security breach. Let's say, later down the line, a potential investor asks, "What's happened in the past six months that you do not want me to know about?"

You have positioned yourself for success when you can honestly say, "Well, we had a reverse due diligence conducted and found a security breach. Not proud of that. But I *am* proud of having invested in the reverse due diligence and then immediately addressed the security breach as a result. We handled it with our clients in the right way. We were above board and disclosed it to them. And we are happy to say that no client was impacted."

Now, roll forward even farther, when that investor is now your owner. If they ask, "How's everything going?" and you say, "Everything is great," they will trust you. You have established both transparency and a dedication to self-investigation.

POSITION WHAT YOU CANNOT FIX

Sometimes you have problems you just cannot fix, but you still must disclose them to potential partners. These are very different than deal breakers.

Maybe you have technical debt. Wait. Let me explain. Technical debt are the things you know you need to do to keep your systems operational and healthy. Chances are you have been letting it pile up because innovation was much sexier than maintenance. Or similar to delaying costs of technical debt, perhaps you have not invested in a benefits plan and are worried about employee retention. You do not necessarily need to fix these problems before going on the market, but you do not want them to be a surprise. Rather, they can be part of the reason you are seeking private equity in the first place.

Back to technical debt, let's say you have not been able to upgrade your systems because you just have not had the money for it. When you disclose that upfront during a conversation about how you would spend funds if you had them, you are in the early stages of developing a roadmap. But what if you are not even aware you need that? What if it is not until later, after the transaction when your new partner discovers pretty much everything needs upgrading, and there was no part of the investment at the time of the transaction to set aside funds for doing so? I am willing to bet neither side will be pleased to discover there is an unexpected expense—sometimes to the tune of millions of dollars. Nobody wants that kind of surprise.

Another common blind spot is the need to rebuild technology. Most founders are self-aware enough to know when they have outgrown their technology. What they do not always know is whether they can build upon what they have or must start from scratch. No one wants to have to rebuild, so the inclination is always to say it is not necessary. But for a lot of founders, the problem is simply in the unknown. If they have been working in one specific technology for the last fifteen years, building it out, then they have not been involved with other more recent technologies. They do not know what is available. Further, if a founder is the one who built the original technology, there is most likely, and should be, a great deal of pride there and maybe some resistance to change it.

When our services have been engaged in this way, being able to partner with the portfolio company and work together has been a positive experience. That does not mean we do not get some reluctance upfront. It is about experience and perspective. Finding the right partner with a market perspective will bolster your team.

I mention this especially because it is a metaphor for the entire process of partnering with investors: when outside people improve your company, they are not trying to take your job. The right-fit partner is not simply buying your technology but rather your expertise. They need to know why you built the original technology the way you did, which, if you have been successful, is because you were being thoughtful about what the client needed.

On the other hand, what if an investor does not find out that you need a technology rebuild until after the deal is closed? Much like in the case of unexpected expense of upgrading your systems, that money was not budgeted during the investment ask that happened prior to the transaction. So it is a sheer cost to the firm. Worse, you are beginning the partnership in a negative way.

Why am I going on and on about this? Your problems only truly become an issue for your investor when they come as a surprise. Otherwise, they are either areas of growth or illustrations of how you behaved in response. Sometimes though, if you do not demonstrate you are the right fit to lead the company for future growth, the private equity firm will be forced to make that tough call.

HIDE NOTHING

As part of the process you will eventually go through a detailed due diligence, or as some refer to it, the discovery phase. This is no longer practice and can be uncomfortable for founders as it can feel like an intrusion: Strangers come looking at every nook and cranny of the business to discover what is going on.

By the time you are into diligence phase, the private equity company is fairly serious about moving forward. They will have signed a letter of intent (LOI) and will be spending a large amount of money for this discovery to make sure they have as much information as possible. When assessing businesses in the low- to mid-market, private equity firms can spend up to $1M for this phase.

A common mistake made by some founders is to misconstrue the intent of the process. It is not an attempt to discover your company trade secrets or to steal your secret sauce. The purpose is to discover what it takes to run your company and what the private equity firm needs to know before they buy the company. They do not need to find all the problems associated with your company. They merely want a clear line of sight to what they will inherit if they purchase you. Your problems today are their problems tomorrow. Private equity firms hate surprises. As a partner you want the firm to know as much as possible to make informed decisions, so the last thing you want to do is to hide things from them.

The question then becomes just how much do you offer up? Can you say too much or, conversely, too little? The short answer to that question is yes. Answer only what you have been asked, period. Again, they are not trying to steal your secrets. At the same time, if they wind up buying your competitor instead of you, they will not be able to unknow whatever you told them, so do not offer up more than they ask. Broadly, you need to address items that are pertinent to the running and operation of servicing clients.

You will want to talk about the current state of your key personnel, including any desire for changes that you are looking to make. It is not uncommon for them to ask for the resumes of all key individuals, so they can get a feel for the depth and pedigree of skills of the people on your team. This is an opportunity to discuss any gaps in skills, or more important, overreliance you have on any one individual. These are common problems, especially for small companies, and exactly the kind a private equity partner can solve.

When it comes to clients, it is vitally important to be as honest and open as possible. For the initial Confidential Information Memorandum (CIM) or pitch deck, you will most likely have pulled together a list of your top ten or twenty clients and the amount of revenue each contributes to your bottom line. These are very important to the buyer, because this shows the financial health and liquidity of the company. They will also ask for your list of at-risk clients.

If any client is in jeopardy—for example, at risk of not renewing or has an ongoing issue with the service or quality that is creating tension with your relationship—then this should be highlighted. This gives the private equity firm an opportunity to make its own judgment about whether this is a systemic problem or an isolated case. If there will be a hole in revenue, the firm will factor that into its risk. The reasons for client losses over the years are clues to a possible remedy. A buyer's plan for the company may make these clients winnable again.

As part of the buying process, the private equity firm will put together financial plans for how much debt your company can handle, how much liquidity is there, etc. It will rely on a certain amount of cash flow and renewable income from your clients to be able to fund expansion, new development, or new hires. Therefore, it is vitally important to disclose anything that would change those figures. Do not hide anything that could come back to haunt you.

As you think about the current technology and systems you have in place to service clients, you need to be honest as to how well these systems operate in the field. Again, you want to paint a healthy picture, but not one so far from the truth that it will hurt you post-transaction. (This is why it's so important to do your own tech due diligence in advance, so you can speak honestly!)

If you made bold statements about your technology and then it turns out that it needs restarting every hour or requires a huge amount of effort to keep it running, you have disingenuously positioned your platform. Over the years, I have worked with many founder/owners who did not even know the efforts their IT team was making to keep up appearances. Also beware of overstating the quality of your data. As tempting as it is to inflate those numbers, there is no gain in overinflating this area, especially if they are perceiving a value in that data where there is none.

A final distinction that is worth noting during this process is the ownership of the data. Do not presume that just because you are holding data in your database that it is legally yours to do with as you please. Depending on the terms and conditions on how you collected that data, it may only be of use for a limited time. Some augmented, third-party data may not be yours at all, but merely licensed for a specific use.

A good technical due diligence will ask certain questions that feel like they have come out of left field. For example, they may ask if you have had any major outages or security breaches in the past twelve months. Respond to these questions truthfully, as they may be answered by others through other processes (for example, public searches of client testimonials). The reason these are asked is to see what exposure the buyer may have and learn how you managed the issue at the time. It is very rare for a company to say they have had no problems in the last twelve months, so the absence of a problem will probably raise more questions than it answers.

The purpose of this discovery is to make sure the buyer has a true understanding of the company. As I have said many times, the key to a good private equity partnership is all about relationships. How you interact with the buyer prior to a transaction is a litmus test for how you will engage post-transaction. Therefore, you and your team should be genuine to illustrate the sort of partner you will be long term.

In the past, I have seen private equity firms walk away from deals because they got a feeling that the people they were interacting with prior to the transaction were not being open or honest. In every email, phone call, and meeting, they are assessing the people in front of them and asking themselves, "Is this someone I can trust as we grow this company?" (You should be doing the same! More on this in the next chapter.) They have a responsibility to their limited partners and to their fund to make sure that every purchase is as successful as possible.

In short, it is vitally important that you do not hide anything or misrepresent something that will come out later. All that will do is undermine the deal.

CLOSING THOUGHTS

As painful as this process may feel or seem at the time, honorable private equity firms are not there to find problems just so they can discount the price. Quite the opposite, they want an honest appraisal of the current state, so everyone is going in with eyes wide open. No one expects everything to be perfect or even necessarily cutting edge. What they do expect is honesty. If problems do arise, price adjustments may occur. If all are honest on both sides of the table, those adjustments will be fair. Now, of course, some firms may use this process to undercut you—but that only means you did not find the right-fit partner.

What is interesting about this new world you are looking to enter is that when a company becomes a portfolio with other companies within a private equity fund, you may find yourself going through what is effectively a medical checkup each and every year. Think of it like a corporate healthcare plan that mandates a medical checkup each year as part of its wellness program. The private equity firm does not want to wait until the next sale to discover any problems. They are looking to solve the problems as they come up long before they become a significant issue, like in preventative medical care.

You have an opportunity to do the same before your first sale to private equity by executing a reverse due diligence. If there is only one thing that you get from this book, then let it be the value of running towards feedback. For that feedback, you need to seek independent outside advice, someone who will come and evaluate a specific area and basically give you a state of the union. Are you going in the right direction? Are you utilizing and adhering to industry standards? Do you have the right tools for the job? Could you be doing things differently? Could you be doing things more cost effectively?

When you pay for due diligence yourself, you know you are getting honest answers—and all the answers. If a private equity firm pays someone to perform a due diligence, and then the investors walk away as a result, you may never know why. Without that information, how can you improve yourself for a future sale? You cannot align with another entity without first understanding the lengths and shapes of your own lines. That is half of the process.

Now you may think that the cost of such a review or checkup outweighs the benefits—for smaller companies that may be true. But many times I have been part of a due diligence where the founder has turned around and said, "I wish I had known this before now." In those cases, I have to remind them that they only had to ask.

What now? You know your boat is seaworthy and navigable, as well as what improvements it needs. Now you are ready to use all of that information to determine what you want in an Admiral.

PAUSE, BREATHE

Here is when you take a moment to check yourself. You have done a lot of research and self-reflection to get to this point, to determine whether or not your company should seek private equity partnership. You have been thinking long and hard about the future and wondering at what point to start this courtship to find the right private equity partner. First, pause to reflect. Is this the right time for you?

Some good news: There is no immediate rush. Six months here, six months there is not going to make a whole lot of difference, so do not feel you are pressured into making an immediate decision. Assuming there is not a life event that is somewhat forcing your hand, you will have the luxury to pick the time that is right for you. You will need to think long and hard if this is the path you want to go down.

Now is the time for introspection. Some of the questions that you may have already asked yourself (which is why you are reading this book in the first place) may include:

- Have I taken the company as far as I can?
- Is it time to let new energy take the company through its next growth?
- As I look to the next big growth area, do I have the capital and expertise to properly execute?
- Have I included all who should benefit from the anticipated wealth creation?

- Should I start thinking about retirement or taking a lesser role?
- Has my succession plan changed as family members step away from the company?
- Could I realize some of the value of the company to create a more secure future for my family?

These are all natural questions and you should not feel guilty about realizing some value for your efforts while setting the stage for those who will come behind you to reap their own benefits.

If you have a spouse or partner, he or she should be the first person you bounce these ideas off of. He or she is the person who knows you the best and has seen firsthand the passion that has driven you to wake up early every morning and go to bed late each night. More likely than not, this person has sacrificed the most as you have built your vision.

If that goes well, the next set of people you want to discuss this with is your most trusted management team. They know the business and the current state of things. You want to observe their reaction to this potential change of course. Are they excited or nervous?

It is important to have a frank and honest conversation. Do not hijack an existing management meeting. Instead, call a special meeting, ideally off site away from the daily noise of operations where people can feel free to think through the implications of your new idea.

Like you, more likely than not, they are new to the private equity space and will have a ton of logistical questions. (*Feel free to buy them a copy of this book as a primer.*) The key to this communication is being completely open and transparent about your motivations.

Once you have your management team up to speed, you all need to figure out collectively when the time is right to start the process.

I want to leave our sailing metaphor again and return to selling a house. I use this analogy constantly when talking to founders about this particular stage of the process. You and your management team need to decide if your house is ready to be shown. (Are there any repairs that you could tackle that will remove potential friction from a would-be buyer? Are there seasonal considerations that should be taken into account?)

Once you have reached the stage of knowing you wish to sell, you need to bring in the experts to walk you through the logistics. In this world, the "realtor" is usually an investment banker or mergers & acquisitions' expert. These are the people who will guide you through the complete process, getting all the necessary information from you so they can produce the materials that will attract the right buyers. I will go through each of these steps in more detail in later chapters, but for the moment, I want to concentrate on that initial "go" state.

In the house selling analogy, finding the right realtor can be as important as finding the right buyer. You will want to find someone that has a good track record of positioning companies like yours and successfully closing the transactions to the right buyers.

First, reach out to your accountant or bank manager. If you utilize the services of one of the top twenty accountancy firms in the country, they will have experience in this process and will be able to recommend several mergers & acquisitions' experts that specialize in your area. Failing that, your bank will most definitely be able to recommend someone. Do not rush this stage. Choosing your representative for this process can make a world of difference. (I suggest you read *The $100 Million Exit: Your Roadmap to the Ultimate Payday* by Jonathan Brabrand.) You will also need legal counsel, specializing in corporate purchases, and a good tax advisor who can guide you through your tax liability as you negotiate various avenues.

An investment transaction may only happen once or twice in the life of a business or entrepreneur. The best mergers and acquisitions attorneys will navigate this rare opportunity as smoothly and efficiently as possible. Find an attorney with a deep understanding of mergers & acquisitions case law, customs, and terminology who also has knowledge of your particular situation, risk tolerance, and transaction goals. Lisa Hedrick, partner at Hirschler, a law firm in Richmond, Virginia, focuses on mergers & acquisitions involving privately held middle market companies. Like most things, the earlier you engage your attorney, the better. How much earlier than before finding your private equity partner? In speaking with Hedrick for this book, she advises, "Engagement one to two years prior to a transaction allows me the opportunity to work with the business owners on tax planning or transaction incentives for employees. Involvement six months before a transaction gives me the chance to work with a business to review books and records from a legal perspective to facilitate an easy diligence process." Six months to two years? Be prepared.

Remember in chapter 1 when I advised you to know your story as a founder before seeking private equity partnership? Your legal advisor should know it too. Hedrick adds, "As the possibility of an investment transaction becomes more certain, I prefer to actively participate in the negotiation of any confidentiality agreement, letter of intent, or term sheet, in order to ensure that the key items of importance for my client are agreed to before the client is committed to a greater spend of time and money to pursue a transaction."

The key to success is that when you pick up the phone or arrange that first meeting with your mergers & acquisitions' advisor, it is with the support of your team.

CHAPTER 4

RECOGNIZE YOUR IDEAL ADMIRAL

Often we talk to founders who think it does not matter which private equity firm invests in them because money is money. That assumption could not be further from the truth. A racing craft does not need an Admiral with experience running cargo. The lone-wolf DIY sailor does not want an Admiral who is controlling. And no one wants to live on a boat with an Admiral who is arrogant or sleeps through crew meetings.

Remember, you are looking for alignment, not just money. To find alignment, you must investigate much more than what your business needs to grow and how much money a private equity firm is offering to support that. This chapter is all about ways to perform a due diligence of sorts on your potential partners. Remember that this is a two-way street. Just because someone wants to acquire you, that does not mean you want to be acquired by them.

Before you put on your gumshoe hat, it is time for a little

more self-reflection. Unless you know what is fundamentally important to you, you cannot assess whether or not a potential investor is a fit.

KNOW YOUR NEEDS

Make sure you can articulate value: both your personal values and belief systems, as well as the value proposition of your business. Those will inform the next thing you need to articulate: your strategic vision for growing your company.

Consider the following when determining your strategic growth vision.

- In what ways do you want to protect your employees and clients that are nonnegotiable?
- Depending on what your company needs supported, determine whether you want to align with a firm in your industry or with a firm that has experience with your company's specific need.
- Do you want a partner who will offer actionable advice, or just one who will give you money and leave it to you to grow your business alone? If the former, seek out advisors who will give you candid feedback and whose skills complement rather than replicate your own.
- Make sure potential investors understand exactly what your value proposition is. It could be that the firm would consider you a widget, a product to buy, whereas you would say, "No, I provide a service."
- Have the metrics to support your value proposition. I asked Nasser Chanda, CEO of Paymerang to share some of his advice about preparing for investment.

He says, "Not all entrepreneurs think about key metrics, but those are important things to communicate to potential buyers. Understand your clients, product by customer, sales model, pipeline, and how often you close leads." (Curious? We will talk more on the importance of key metrics in chapter 7.)

- Know who your key competitors are and understand why your company is more attractive than your competitors. Researching your own competitors is no different or less important than researching your potential investors.
- Be aware that your strategic vision may evolve. Especially if this is your first time with private equity, you may change your mind about your goals as you learn more about what a partnership will look like. I worked with a founder once who did not know until she started speaking with private equity firms, that her company had insight into an entirely new market. I have also seen founders who thought they wanted to leave after the sale, but then, during the process, decided they wanted to stay. Be prepared to articulate how your story is evolving.

CONSIDER STRENGTHS NONNEGOTIABLE

The second time Royall & Company went through an investment transaction process, we specifically needed more sales support. Bill did not just have his name on the side of the building. His leadership, values, and culture were felt in every aspect of the business, most profoundly in sales. When he started to step back, he still remained chairman of the board. We knew that moving forward, we needed a right-fit partner who could support us in selling more of what we had figured out was really working for colleges and universities. Further, because Bill had so effectively instilled his vision in his C-Suite—we as a management team were largely in charge of deciding which private equity firm to partner with.

But what kind of sales support would grow our business? Our main objective was to remain a trusted partner with our clients, to continue creating value for them. We needed to make sure that whoever we selected would allow us to sell to new clients in a way that further developed that kind of trust, while also not distracting us from continuing to serve our existing clients.

Let's say, hypothetically, that we had been approached by a private equity firm that had sold businesses in the automobile industry and made millions of dollars. And they said, "We think we can help you sell more to colleges and universities because we have figured it out in the automobile industry. Even though it is slightly different, we know it will work and we want you to do it that way, to achieve exponential growth."

But we knew that the way we engaged directly and personally with presidents of schools was one of our biggest strengths. Just because that firm has experience increasing sales, if they wanted us to step away from the fundamental pillar of the way we do business, then they would not be the right fit.

We needed a firm that would say, "We are interested in the education space because we believe in the service of that space, and we think the way you engage with presidents is the gold-star standard. We have developed a plan to increase sales that is respectful of your history and in keeping with your goals."

These are the sorts of factors we considered when making the decision ultimately to partner with CHS Capital. My point here is that we would not have known how to choose and what questions to ask if we had not really taken the time to investigate our own goals as well as our strengths. Your strengths should be nonnegotiable. (A word of caution: private equity sees a lot of business proposals, and as you probably would guess, every single one of them says, "We are different," "We are special," or "We are unique," whether talking about their customer service, product, or another strength. While it is, as I have said, important to know your strengths, remember that many founders also have great products and great customer service, so you may not technically be all that "unique." Be careful with the language you use to express your strengths. The last thing you want is for someone at a private equity firm to roll their eyes while reading your proposal.)

Another example comes from Carl Hewitt, co-founder of Decisions, along with Heath Oderman, who are also clients of MacLaurin Group. Decisions provides technology for automation of key business processes and business rules, making the business logic accessible to non-programming staff. In ten years, they have grown their business such that their technology is used directly by companies on almost all continents, ranging from small or mid-sized companies to over a dozen Fortune 500 companies, all from right here in the Commonwealth of Virginia. They have succeeded in large part because of the strength of the company's culture and the founders' dedication to developing and maintaining that culture.

You could be the most brilliantly talented person in your discipline, but if you do not buy into that culture, Hewitt is not going to hire you. For Decisions, culture is a nonnegotiable strength. When he was searching for his right-fit private equity partner, he made sure to align with one that also valued culture and understood it as one of the keys to Decisions's success. I recently joined one of the company's town halls with the entire team at Decisions and was blown away (if not surprised) by what they and Aldrich Capital Partners have accomplished together. As Decisions has grown the company to more than 175 employees, it continues to embody the culture Hewitt and Oderman set out to build.

EVERYONE MUST ROW IN THE SAME DIRECTION

It is also important to think about how procedures and processes might change depending on your investor.

After Royall & Company's third transaction, we went from private to public. That hugely affected my day-to-day operations as a leader. Bill was known for culminating a contract with a handshake. It is completely reasonable and easy to understand that in a public company that has the potential to be more complex and challenging.

In a public company, you will need to consider additional layers of complexities, such as having to report quarterly numbers. How does that impact a business with cyclical upticks?

Please do not misinterpret me here—quarterly earnings are important. Founders and entrepreneurs who experience a more cyclical revenue stream may have a deeper appreciation for what I am trying to articulate.

My question for you is, what approach best fits your leadership style? Do you see yourself seeking private equity investments or aspiring to be a public company? There is no wrong answer as long as you are finding a right fit. Look at the track record of the firm—many private equity firms never take companies public. It is much harder to do because there is a "lock-up" period. A lot can happen during that period (three months to six months), and the deal may fail to go through. These are important scenarios to hypothesize in advance of a transaction.

UNDERSTAND EXPECTATIONS THAT WILL BE MADE OF YOU

Chances are you will be staying on and you will have good days and bad days together. Setting expectations up front is important to ensure the good days outweigh the bad. What are the expectations from you, if you are staying on? Ask questions about the reporting structure before choosing your new boss or bosses. How and when is the best way to work together and communicate with one another?

An important part of communication will be to determine your expectations during board meetings and board presentations. The private equity firm will have its own cadence and expectations about how to run a board meeting and what is needed from you prior, during, and after a board meeting. A critical component in that process is setting clear expectations on decision-making.

PERFORM A DUE DILIGENCE ON *THEM*

Once you know what you want and need, research potential investors to make sure they align with you. I will
discuss the importance of researching the firm's operating
partners and advisors, where founders of the firm's other
portfolio companies are now, and how culture changed at
the firm's other portfolio companies. First, here's a primer
on the three things that investors can provide to you as a
company owner or founder: money, advice, and introductions. The easiest of the three to diligence is the money,
but there are shades of grey here as well.

When it comes to money, there are three general types of
private equity investors. First are the growth-equity investors, who take minority positions in your company, with
ownership stakes less than 50 percent. Growth equity is
the right choice when a founder wants to put some money
in their pocket, or when the founder requires capital to
grow the business. Growth-equity investors are minority
owners, so they cannot tell you, as a founder, what to do—
they can only make suggestions. Sounds good in theory,
the devil is in the details of the letter of intent. Growth-
equity investors often include language that gives them
additional control if your business goes off track. So be
careful. Growth investors are the best bet if you, as the
founder, still want to run the company. You will have
majority ownership of your company, so valuation is not
as important.

Buyout investors take controlling interest in your business—owning more than 50 percent. Buyout investors
have control of your company from the outset of their
investment. In the event of a disagreement over strategy

or direction, they hold all of the cards. Buyout investors often do not let the founder run the company after their investment. They are the preferred choice for founders who want to step away from the day-to-day running of the company. Because you are selling more of your company, valuation is more critical. When done right, however, you can get two bites of the apple. The best buyout shops often give you greater return when they sell the company than they did when they bought it.

It is important to note this only happens if you put money back into the company. Be cautious of the structure and ask questions when making a decision to invest. Private equity firms usually set up deals to allow them to get their payouts first. In order for you to also get a payout, you must roll in a decent amount of your equity. Keep in mind it is not always about the number of shares as that is only the numerator in the equation. Make sure you understand the denominator too in order to fully understand the percentage of your ownership. (Owning a hundred shares of a total pool of a thousand shares is far different than owning a hundred shares of a total pool of a million shares. You know this even before the math.)

Leveraged-buyout groups are the third type of private equity investor. They use a combination of cash and debt to buy your company. ("Regular" buyout shops use debt as well, but debt is not a core part of their investment process.) Leveraged-buyout shops use higher ratios of debt, and they depend on the cash flow of the business to service that debt. You will be giving up control, and you will want to take as much cash upfront as possible. You will not be running the business and, if it goes sideways, the debt holders will take control of your company. There are variations of all three of these types of investors, so you will need to pay close attention to the term sheet. Regardless of which type of partner is the right fit for you, it is important to understand their success rate with previous investments.

Now that you know what kind of financial relationship you want to have with a firm, let's consider those other two assets they bring to the table: advice and introductions. Sometimes firms want to diversify their portfolios. In doing so, they are looking specifically for a company that is not in a business previously in their portfolio. You cannot assume the investors will know your industry. Perhaps that does not matter to you because you just need someone who has expertise in growing businesses, period. But money is relatively easy—advice and introductions, not so much.

The best investors focus on particular types of companies, and you will want to choose investors that have history in your specific industry. Founders of software companies should select investors that have experience owning software companies—ditto with healthcare businesses or manufacturing or consumer goods. Avoid partnering with investors who are newbies to your business type. Why? Advice and introductions from newbies are not very useful to you as a founder. When you talk to founders and CEOs of a firm's other portfolio companies—as I will implore you to do later in the chapter—ask whether that private equity group adds real value beyond money. Further, keep in mind that it is not just the deal partner who should have experience in your industry. Say, for example, the deal partner is the only software investor in the fund. That can become a problem, as the other partners may not understand your business.

There are a couple more major factors to consider before diving into thorough investigations of potential private equity partners:

- Beware the potential partner who wants to change everything about your company. That is not a partner. You want someone who will build on what you have and be a sounding board for you along the way.
- Beware of hubris, of anyone claiming to know how to do what you do better. It is far too early in the process for anyone to truly know how to support your business. Someone who says, "I have a better idea," could not possibly have actual buy-in for your idea.

Now, here are some ways to perform a more thorough due diligence on your potential partners' personnel and histories. Throughout, remember that your reference checks should not solely focus on what went right, but also look for the times when things did not go well. Do not evaluate your future partners on their best days; evaluate them on the people they become on their worst days. If you have an uncomfortable gut feeling, have multiple meetings before making a decision that will tie you together for a long time.

And make sure you understand how the private equity firm may have weathered previous economic downturns. Private equity firms do not keep money laying around. In an economic downturn, when the firm turns to its limited partners to collect their pledged amount, do you know the track record of limited partners to honor their investment commitments?

BACKGROUND CHECK THE PRIVATE EQUITY FIRM'S PEOPLE

Start by getting to know the main partners of the firm. Their voices carry a lot of weight in decisions made by the firm. Determine their interests and where they focus priorities and time. Are their philanthropic activities in line with yours or the culture of your team? Evaluating how they prioritize their own resources can foreshadow how they will prioritize and make investments on your behalf or support you in doing so. Determine on what boards they sit, their roles on the boards, their interests, and what they would bring to the table beyond financial investment.

Look at the firm's outcomes in previous partnerships. Has it been successful with portfolio companies that are similar to yours? In the scenario of multiple investments, or reinvestments, what are the returns? You can find out what portfolio companies they held and whether or not they sold at a loss by checking PR newswires or picking up the phone. Ask the founders of other portfolio companies if, with this firm, they were able to hit the goals they set out to achieve.

Do you want someone who will collaborate, provide feedback, and offer advice? Or do you just want someone to fund you to go it alone? Advice and introductions may come in the form of operating partners. What skills do their operating partners have and how will they work with you post transaction? The best groups have operations people who provide actionable advice and partnerships.

These advisors provide you with the support you need to grow in your new and expanded role.

It is important to understand the skills a private equity firm's operating partners have and how they will work with you post transaction. Are the management teams within the private equity firm's current portfolio happy and feel they are being surrounded by support post transaction?

Research the private equity firm's advisors. Call other private equity firms or founders who have worked with this advisor in the past. What is their success record? How is their integrity? Do you have nondisclosure agreements in place? The advisors are not just a mechanical part of this process. They can hold a lot of sway.

Keep this in mind when choosing your own advisors. Make sure your advisors can be trusted if they find themselves in the position of advising both sides. Will everyone be comfortable working with them in that case? Do they have enough integrity to, as they say in real estate, represent both the seller and the buyer? We find ourselves in this position quite a bit, and our clients trust us to be the best advisor we can be to each party.

Finally, step back and remember that sometimes the best way to due diligence a private equity firm's personnel is to observe how they treat others in the process besides you. The level of respect the private equity firm extends to you should look the same as it does to those already a part of the team.

How do the partners at the private equity firm interact with their associates—those individuals pushing the forward momentum in the process—as the deal is being formed? Is this how you would treat someone on your team? Ask yourself if that is how you would want to be treated as a team member. See where I am going here? If the transaction is successful, you will be treated as a part of the team.

CASE STUDY: OPERATING PARTNERS AND THE "VALLEY OF ANGUISH"

In the case of Royall & Company, Chicago Growth Partners brought to the table an operations team that was literally boots on the ground, not just advice. When I asked Jim Milbery to recall his boots-on-the-ground approach for scaling technology at Royall, Milbery recalled, "Bill Royall had always imagined building a software platform that automated some of the core tasks of the business. We brought some of the technical expertise that was needed to help turn that vision into reality." That technical expertise included my first introduction to Alan Williamson.

If you have had the opportunity to work with Milbery or listen to one of his podcasts, you know he has a wonderful way of disarming you with self-deprecation. Milbery went on to say (in a very strong Boston accent), "My initial contribution was telling them that this would be a cake-walk—it wasn't. I told them that we could deliver on this vision in less than two years—we couldn't. I reassured him that it would all work out in the end—it did." Wicked awesome.

The team at Royall & Company adopted Milbery's standard visual model used to describe the life cycle of all large-scale projects. Satisfaction is on the X-axis and Time is on the Y-axis. It starts with a single point on a line graph showing the kickoff point. Initially, the line moved up and to the right as everyone got excited about the direction in which we were all headed. As we dug into the new platform, the line dropped dramatically down past the original starting point and then flattened out. This is fondly referred to as the *Valley of Anguish,* where everyone is disillusioned and wished that we had never started the project in the first place.

The Valley of Anguish is a real thing. To translate it to our sailing analogy, this is when your ship is out at sea in the middle of a storm, and you are tired and weary, but there is little time for rest. This is when you get the real value of having investors with operational expertise. They can point you to the lighthouse beaming on the shoreline.

The advisors were not employees, so we could not fire them (thankfully). Slowly but surely, the line began to move up and to the right, eventually moving far above the original starting point. (As much as Milbery still pokes fun at me about this, I created an "excitement committee" to help keep everyone focused on delivering for clients while navigating the business through the Valley of Anguish. We all knew that we had taken the right path when everybody stopped complaining about the new platform and started taking credit for the project and insisting they had been *believers all along.* To their credit, everyone stayed with it, and together we delivered on Bill's original vision. (We had a name for that project, which will come up later. The name was "Royfoo." Don't ask. Bill hated it. Sorry, Bill.)

As for Milbery, we named a conference room after him, and Royall & Company's engineering team used that conference room when they needed to professionally debate—by which I mean argue—about some-thing. That was the best way to show appreciation to Milbery, who welcomes a good debate, in the spirit of partnership and boots on the ground. You want a partner who has experienced the Valley of Anguish and come out on the other side successful. Remember, it is all about the journey.

BACKGROUND CHECK IMPACTS ON CULTURE AND THE WORKPLACE

Your company is going to change. Change is what you want, after all; this is not a bank loan. What you do not want are major changes to your company's workforce or culture that ultimately undermine your larger goals. As you know, the leaders of a company set the tone and rhythm. If the senior leadership of your company largely stays the same, then you are likely to have a seamless transition. If, on the other hand, some of the senior leadership changes, that may have significant impacts on productivity and overall employee well-being. The question you must ask yourself is whether your employees can tolerate such a change. Will this transaction change the overall productivity, possibly impacting client delivery? Investigate what happened at other companies in a private equity firm's portfolio.

I have seen companies go from being customer-driven organizations, whereby no matter what time of day it was, the clients' needs were always served, to the other extreme where clients' needs were only served between 9 a.m. and 5 p.m., even if a call for help came through at 5:05 p.m. The employees felt disengaged and there was no incentive or desire to put in the extra effort to make the client success-ful—all because of a change in leadership, and therefore, in company values. The well-being of your employees post transaction is paramount to the success of your company.

As part of your due diligence on your potential new private equity partner, you want to discover how much staff turnover their portfolios have experienced in the first eighteen months of their involvement. Start by asking how many executives have rolled out in the first twelve months. The executives of the portfolio will have the most touch points with the private equity partners and they are the ones who will feel the biggest change. If there is a higher turnover than usual, this signifies an amount of change from the historical way of working to a point where they felt they could not continue forward.

This is particularly important for a company coming into this space for the first time, as most of the executives are incentivized only on the subsequent transaction and not in this transaction. That means the situation was intolerable enough that they did not want to hang in there while waiting for their payday. While this is a rare occurrence, it does happen. If one executive leaves, that is not necessarily an indication that the whole culture completely changes. If, however, a large percentage of the executive team leaves, you have to ask "why?" It is important to note the one exception to executive turnover: the CFO position. As the company scales, it is more common to go through CFOs every few years as they tend to be "best" at businesses of a certain stage and size.

If, as the current founder and leader, you are wishing to step aside or step away—or are being told to step away—then a new CEO has to be installed. This person will come with their own culture and their own personality that will trickle down into the rest of the company. Given the importance and influence a CEO plays, the private equity firm will have the major say when it comes to choosing that person. That does not mean you are completely ignored, but your influence is diminished. Still, if you care about the future of your company and your employees, you want to make sure the right person is selected.

You want to know what sort of metrics they are looking for and what personalities they generally prefer in their CEOs. It is very easy to find executive bios for CEOs of their companies. As you read through these (and their corresponding LinkedIn profiles), see if there are common traits or types they tend towards. Ideally, ask to be introduced to one or two CEOs, so you can ask direct questions and determine if that style of CEO would work for your company.

Every decision management makes is felt by the employees at some point. Your employees are the foundation of your company. You want to gauge if the foundations of the portfolio companies shifted significantly after their transactions, enough to cause visible cracks. Employee turnover within the first eighteen months is a good metric to investigate. If it is higher than normal, that may merit a closer inspection.

Look at services online to get a feel for how employees are conducting themselves publicly. Sites such as Glassdoor offer forums for anonymous feedback on companies' cultures and environment. I will caution against putting too much weight behind Glassdoor, as it is a little like the exit interview and is sometimes treated as a means to vent frustration and anger without context. That said, if there is a higher than normal turnover of employees, you may see a common thread as to why they have sought opportunities elsewhere. Do not give attention to the one angry rant. Do look for the trends, whether positive or negative.

Other social media services such as LinkedIn, Twitter, and Facebook can offer insight. Doing quick searches on historical portfolio companies can sometimes yield a huge amount of information. Remember you are not always looking for bad information. You are also looking for positive information to celebrate. Are they doing more or less community service activities? Is there a general sense of pride and excitement around recruiting?

Your goal is simply to discover how the transaction impacted the workforce of the portfolio company. Take this information and play it against your own workforce to determine whether this firm would be a good or bad fit.

FIND OUT WHERE PREVIOUS FOUNDERS ARE NOW

Even if you are the very first company in a brand-new fund for a brand-new private equity company, the founders and partners of the private equity firm will still have worked with other companies historically. That means there is a track record to review to determine how founders fared under their stewardship.

One of the goals of a private equity firm is to grow wealth for both fund and portfolio shareholders alike. When you first enter this world, it is tempting to take all the money on offer. If you are looking to stay active with the portfolio in any shape or form, it is wise to reinvest some of that money back into the portfolio.

At New Harbor Capital, 100 percent of the founders they invested in have turned around and invested in the firm's fund or have stayed on as advisors—even after those founders exited. This shows a huge confidence in the private equity firm. (As Adam Coffey noted in his book, it is very common for this type of reinvestment to yield far greater returns than the initial payout would have resulted. I can speak from personal experience that investing back into a portfolio company after its acquisition has been the best way to put my money to work.)

As you perform your own due diligence on your new potential partners, you want to understand how many of their portfolios (both past and present) that are similar to yours (founder-led, staying on) rolled money back into the fund. Find out roughly what percentage that was. This provides insight into the value the private equity firm places on this type of commitment.

Ask questions about founders' other decisions. If one stepped away after the first transaction, find out whether or not they intended to stay on, and if so, try to find out why they stepped away or, worse, why they were pushed out. The reason might not always be cause for alarm. Perhaps a founder misunderstood the nature of private equity partnerships (or maybe they did not have the insights that you have of reading this book).

Just like with any new journey, things are always great at the start as excitement and anticipation build. The story and success of any new discovery can change as the years pass by. In your investigations, focus less on recent founders in the firm's portfolio and more on founders who have been through a number of transactions and are still connected to the private equity firm in one way or another. The most common way a founder may still be involved after a number of transactions with a private equity firm is to continue to invest in subsequent funds of the firm. This is a clear signal that the firm has been successful historically, and the founders continue to trust in the firm's leadership ability to make good and rewarding investments.

Founders who wish to remain a little more hands-on might also be invited to sit on the private equity firm's board of advisors. This is a collection of seasoned successful business people who are there to guide the firm's investments. Some advisors will get involved in new companies coming into the portfolio by either taking a seat on the board or taking on the chairman role. Drawing on their input is highly encouraged. Therefore, before entering into a partnership, you want to evaluate the roster of experts. Ideally, their industry experience aligns with yours and your needs. Ask current CEOs of the firm's portfolio companies how active their advisory boards are and if their experience is indeed accessible and shared.

Remember you are entering a partnership. Your success is their success. Use every resource possible when choosing the right-fit partner.

EVERYTHING IS UP FOR EVALUATION

Dinner and cocktails is when we relax and get to know each other after a long day of meetings—the management meetings and due diligence are over, right? No. Be keenly aware that the private equity firm is anticipating that you will let down your guard and reveal your true core values. This is the opportunity for you to assess their values as well. There are a great deal of things you can determine about one's value system at the dinner table.

The level of respect the private equity firm's representatives extend to the wait staff will foreshadow how they treat those in service to them, such as the facilities team responsible for taking care of your office space each day. (For that matter, do you know the names of those who provide security for your building? Those who provide maintenance service? Cleaning services? Do you show your appreciation? You should.)

Watch how your potential partners treat everyone. Is there a level of respect or a barking of orders? Most likely you will be interacting with accountants, lawyers, and other service providers (such as those who provide a service of technical due diligence or outline your technology vision and architecture, which are favorite examples of mine, wink wink). Also assess how the firm's representatives treat these service providers. In every interaction, whether with the waitstaff or a CEO, you want to observe a sense of partnership in the interaction.

IN TURBULENT TIDES, YOUR VALUES ARE YOUR LIFE VEST

Right. You get it. Take the time to research your potential investors. And please, always research potential investors *before* walking into a meeting with them.

I once sat down with a founder who was very salesman-like. This person's plan was to border on dishonesty in order to impress. There is a world in which some investors are attracted to that kind of bluster and confidence. But if this founder had taken the time to research me, they would have known the most important things to me are transparency, honesty, and integrity. By failing to understand me, they wasted both my time and their own.

I have also met with plenty of founders who were incredibly successful but were also jerks. I do not care how much money we might make in partnering together, if you are an asshole (and yes, I would say that even in front of my mom or grandmother), then I do not wish to work with you. And if they had asked absolutely anyone who has ever worked with me, they would have known that.

Remember that you are aligning much more than financial goals.

CLOSING THOUGHTS

Often we think about private equity as a win-or-lose game. To introduce another analogy, people sometimes believe that there is only so much of the pie to go around for everybody. I want you to think about private equity as a way of baking a bigger pie.

That way of thinking is the difference between choosing money or choosing alignment. Sometimes choosing to receive less money now means you will all make more money later, because you are growing in the right way as a result of truly being aligned. It is just like what we were discussing in chapter 2 about choosing the right client: money is not worth it if the baggage that comes with it will distract you from your long-term goals. You are going to have enough distractions as it is.

Now, you may be asking, *How much does all of this advice matter if only one firm wants to buy my company? Even if I am not so sure about the values of the advisors, am I really going to walk away? Does that happen? In what circumstances do you advise that?* I have two responses. First, remember you are choosing who will own your company on the other side. Full ownership. If you are slightly uncomfortable now, you will be much more uncomfortable later. Second, if you only have one offer, now is not your time to sell. You have no leverage, which is a terrible place to be. You need to ask yourself why you want to sell right now and make sure it would not be better to wait instead.

Now you know how to choose your Admiral. And once you have done so, it will be time to set sail and stay your course. But first, you need to make sure that during this extended, time-consuming process, you do not leave your boat unattended. In the next chapter, we will discuss ways to keep the distractions from affecting your business and your clients.

PRIVATE EQUITY 101: HOW LONG TO HOLD AND WHEN TO SELL AGAIN?

Once entering into this wonderful world of private equity, one thing is for sure: at some point in the future, your company will undergo another transaction. Whether it is sold to another private equity firm or becomes part of a larger company as part of a tuck-in, a transaction of some kind will happen. This, of course, is how a fund makes the bulk of its money.

Rarely there is a hard timetable. Instead it is driven by circumstance, and the private equity firm is the expert in knowing how to recognize opportunities. You want to understand the criteria that a given firm looks for as a trigger. The best way you can get a feel for this is to look at their historical transactions and ask what drove each decision. It can be as simple as that the timing was right, the numbers were being made year-on-year, or someone came a-knocking. Conversely, maybe the numbers were not looking as healthy as they should be, and the private equity firm wanted to offload a portfolio company while there was still value in it. Alternately, maybe another private equity firm was better equipped to take the company to the next level.

Timing is sometimes out of the private equity firm's control. I was reminded, when interviewing partners for this book, that when Chicago Growth Partners sold Royall & Company, it was earlier than expected. At the time, not all the partners wished to sell. But the senior partners wanted to raise a new fund and knew that a successful exit from Royall & Company would assist with the raise. Ultimately the decision was made to sell earlier than some preferred.

While it may come as a surprise, it should never be taken personally or feel as a betrayal. They are there to make money for their limited partners in their fund. When you are ultimately an investor in their fund, you will want them to make the very same decisions to maximize your investment.

Upon execution of a transaction, the chances are you will have at least a couple of years with your new partners. Come year three, you need to be on medium alert, that at anytime you could get the call from your partner letting you know they are exploring a transaction. You should be in a state of semi-readiness and, given that you have already gone through it once, subsequent events will be nowhere near as disruptive or stressful.

Some funds act like a typical shopping mall, with anchor stores and lots of surrounding smaller shops, resulting in a healthy mix. In the fund the anchor company is the one that is maybe a little larger than others, continually hitting or exceeding their quarterly projections and proving to be valued at a sum greater than expected. These companies keep the fund as a whole profitable, even as others may not be performing as well as they should. What happens when your company is the jewel in their crown? Depending on the age of the fund, and whether or not any returns have yet to be made, they may look to sell you quicker to provide that large return to their investors, or they could hold onto you longer, while they sell the smaller portfolios.

At the time of a sale, assuming you are being offered to a number of different buyers, you want to understand just how much influence you will have when it comes to choosing your next partner. When first entering this space, you had full control over who that partner was going to be. The next and subsequent times you will have partners sitting beside you on the same side of the table, all making that decision. While the process as a whole will feel a lot easier, you will experience far less control. If you are still actively involved in the company, you will want to know if you have at least a vote or a say on choosing the next partner. It is not necessarily a bad thing if you do not have that much weight in the decision. Trust the private equity firm to know what it is doing. After all, you selected it as your right-fit partner at the start of this journey.

Which brings me to the point where I should mention club deals—transactions with more than one investor. In a club deal, you might have one non-control investor and another investor with controlling interest. There is a good chance they will not be on the same timeline for rounding out their funds. Let's say you are the first deal in a fund for firm A. In three years from now, firm A will need an exit. Let's say this happens alongside an investment from firm B where you are the last deal in their fund, which means they have exhausted their fund and are in a position for a longer hold. This could lead to strategic friction. This is something that often takes founders by surprise. If you are considering a club deal, remember that the alignment the investors share on loving you and your company might not extend any further.

Whatever kind of firm you partner with, when the right opportunity is presented, it will move to sell your company, and it may happen fast. Knowing what this might look like in advance will make all interactions with your new private equity partners much easier.

CHAPTER 5

STAY THE COURSE

You have taken time to assess your boat and yourself, to figure out what you need out of an Admiral. You have taken time to investigate potential Admirals, to determine if they could be right-fit partners. All of that has taken you away from the dock. So who is protecting your vessel? It will not matter what partner you choose, if you have no boat to voyage in.

It can happen before you realize it. You make the mistake of letting yourself become distracted in the process of seeking a private equity partnership. Seeking investment requires an incredible amount of time and stamina. Not only are you tasked with everything we have discussed in this book, but also the nuts and bolts of pitching—creating decks, all of the meetings, and selling, selling, selling. Further, the process of seeking a partnership will affect the way your business runs.

Fortunately, there are steps you can take to mitigate the madness, ensuring that even when you are pulled away, your precious commodity will be surrounded by calm waters. First, embrace transparency with your employees, and especially among your management team. This will squash problems before they arise and also invite support. Second, deputize your management team and delegate so you are not swamped doing it all yourself—and so your boat does not stall out waiting for you to act.

The whole point is having a business to sell and grow once you are on the other side of it. Your clients are counting on it.

TRANSPARENCY FOR SUCCESS OF EVERYONE

I oftentimes get challenged about transparency, especially working in a world of nondisclosures and private transactions. Sometimes certain pieces of information must remain private, or the deal will be in danger of falling apart. Sometimes you will have to sign an NDA so strict it does not even allow you to say you are up for sale. And as a founder, you may not *want* people to know you are up for sale.

To be sure, there are appropriate times and inappropriate times to share information. You should always adhere to the confidentiality expected of you. (One of the reasons we have been successful growing MacLaurin Group is because clients know they can count on us to both honor confidentiality and transparency.) Regardless of the degree of secrecy required, however, there are still ways to diminish fear and increase trust among your employees.

At a minimum, if your employees sense that something is happening behind closed doors and approach you with nervous questions, you should be able to look them in the eyes and tell them they have nothing to worry about. You should explain that you cannot answer their question, but that they can trust you to move the company in directions that will ultimately serve you all better. If you have already developed a culture of transparency and trust, then they will believe you and be motivated to continue working to make your company valuable.

STAGE YOUR TRANSPARENCY

Many founders are inclined to be secretive about the process of seeking private equity partnership. It is a knee-jerk reaction driven by fear. They are scared that their employees will get nervous. My response to that is, "Is there a motive you need to hide?" The only reason to keep everyone in the dark would be if your goal is to sell, exit, and then not care what happens to your employees and clients. But if that were you, you would not still be reading this book.

Your intention, however, is to keep growing the company. You care about what happens to your employees and clients. There are reasons for confidentiality throughout the process as a duty to everyone involved. But for what you can share, it is important to start thinking now, before you begin a process, how and when you will communicate throughout. Thinking through your preferred communication plan after the process begins may be too late.

One simple strategy is to put up welcome signs.

I remember when Royall & Company was seeking investment, and Bill brought the private equity firms in through the front door. He literally put a welcome sign in the lobby, so you knew which firm was talking to management that day. It was born out of a previous practice of Bill's, dating to the early days of the company, when college presidents did not know what to expect from this new kind of marketing and recruitment firm. He did not want them to think of us as a factory, so he invited them to visit and see that our employees were a happy, engaged group who worked in an inspiring and creative environment. The passion with which our employees approached their work and each other was a proxy for how we served our clients.

Welcoming private equity investors in this same way was a celebration of the process, and also Bill's way of being clear that we were looking for the right investor, because growing in the right way was important to our clients and for our employees. Having a welcome sign gives every employee the opportunity to research the firms to find out what they do and, more important, what their values are, which only builds more trust between you and your employees and ultimately commitment from them.

Turns out that Bill was right about those welcome signs. Rob Healy, partner at L Squared Capital, recalls the moment he knew Royall & Company was the right fit:

> "I knew it was the right-fit partnership because of the culture at Royall & Company and the degree to which customer services was 'over the top in every single way and action' from the way a client was picked up from the airport, to the way presentations were an engagement with clients, to

dinners. During the on-site visit with Royall & Company, private equity firms were treated like a client visit, and it was the way Royall made sure I had the experience to feel what Royall did for their clients. Royall was growing. Royall had incredible customer retention, so the story was that it all fit together."

Once Healy had been on-site and saw firsthand the high quality of personal bond everyone had with one another—and that he had experienced himself—he said (in his words), "There was no way we were going to lose the deal."

Knowing how to get the balance between transparency and confidentiality right is tough. I spoke with Jonathan Brabrand, managing director at Transact Capital Partners, and author of *The $100 Million Exit: Your Roadmap to the Ultimate Payday,* to ask him to expand on what I refer to as "staged transparency." Jonathan has twenty years of experience of business owners trusting their exits to him as an investment banker. In his playbook he shares narratives of lessons typically experienced only in confidential conversations and behind closed doors. Jonathan counsels his sell-side clients to take a staged approach to transparency with their employees and other key stakeholders throughout the sale process.

Brabrand and I agree this involves crafting the message as one of excitement around what a new partner will be able to do for the company's future and what new chapters will be created with the involvement of new owners. We also agree how important it is to emphasize that senior management is planning to stay (if that is the case) in order to provide reassurance that there will be a continuity of leadership. Brabrand recommends sharing that message in four stages:

> "First, at the beginning of the process, we share the message with those executives that will need to be involved in the process and will have direct exposure to potential buyers. Just before the marketing process begins, we may also share the message with key salespeople or other market-facing personnel, to prep them in case they hear any rumors in the market. Thirdly, once a buyer has been selected, we communicate with those team members that will be needed to support the due diligence efforts. Finally, at closing, we make the internal announcement to the full employee base, again emphasizing that the sale will create new possibilities for the company and new opportunities for the employees going forward."

Employees will most likely not be familiar with all of the positives associated with a private equity investment. Recall all of the myths we discussed earlier? Chances are, if you do not control the narrative, your employees will fear some version of this myth: *private equity will buy a company, load it up with debt so they can take money out, and then leave it and the employees for dead.* And if you think that your employees do not know that you are selling, then you are fooling yourself, not them.

You as the founder are ultimately the only one who can make the best decision on timing communications. You know your leadership style, your employees, and how communication will best align with your culture and core values. Adam Coffey, of CoolSys, told me he creates YouTube videos to communicate with his employees. At his last company, every employee knew he had plans to sell it three years in advance of when he did. And he communicated why that was a good thing and not a scary thing. He communicated current revenue, earnings before interest, taxes, depreciation, and amortization (EBITDA), and size, and where each measure needed to be in order to sell. So as the company began to hit those numbers, people knew a sale was probably coming. Then, Coffey walked twenty-seven potential partners through the front door. Sound familiar?

But think about the genius of Coffey's plan for a second. He foreshadowed partnership. Even if he had found himself in a situation where he could not bring potential partners in through the front door, he had still established with his employees that he would be seeking private equity partnership once they reached certain benchmarks. Further, he had developed general trustworthiness. So even if his employees began to wonder if something was going on behind closed doors, they would also assume they had no reason to worry about it.

You may be thinking, "I don't want my employees to worry about what will happen in the process and quit. Heck, Kelley, I don't even have the answers for myself at this point." I get it. But by keeping the entire process a secret to everyone, you may wind up creating the very conditions that will lead them to think about leaving.

Even if you have the best intentions—maybe you just do not want to distract your employees—it can still be a self-fulfilling prophecy. For example, while you are seeking partnership, you might not want to hire new employees or make big systems investments, because once you decide who your partner is, the kinds of people you need to hire and the kinds of investments you want to make might be different. Naturally, you will need to put some spending and infrastructure planning on hold.

Say, for example, you need an expanded sales team (and you have for a while). Your employees already know that you are planning to build it out, that there is a million-dollar budget for it, and that you have even held some interviews. But then you start meeting with investors, and one of the private equity firms already has an incredible sales team. If you are not communicating with your management team, and to your employees, they will start asking themselves, "Why are we not hiring? Why is our founder not fulfilling promises? Do we not have a budget? Is the company in trouble? Does our founder no longer care?"

They will know something is happening because your time is now being diverted. But since you are not controlling the dialogue, by sharing information and being transparent about your pursuits, you are letting them create narratives for themselves. Then, instead of focusing on clients and growing your business, they are more worried about what will happen to them.

Your highest valued employees are the ones that are the most marketable. They are the ones you could lose the fastest. Those employees whose jobs are dependent on having a shiny new sales team are going to assume their jobs are no longer needed. If you are not controlling the message from the start of seeking investment, they will have found another job before the process is finished or even begins. But when you are transparent throughout, they will understand that their positions will only grow after investment as a result of partnering with the firm's existing sales team.

Also, consider that a private equity firm, or someone doing market research, could call any of your employees at any time to ask questions about you or the business. Just because you did not set up communications between potential partners and current employees does not mean those communications will not happen. When you have a culture of communication and trust in all of the conversations you can control, you do not have to worry about any of the others happening outside of you.

I have been a part of transactions where there is transparency and where there is not. Transparency is really hard, because you have to be vulnerable. But it is so valuable to do so. You, your team, the private equity firm, and your advisors are making big, high stakes decisions here. If you hold back even a small piece of the puzzle, you will not have all of the data needed to make a decision. Further, you will not have everything you need for everyone to rally behind you. Determine your cadence for staged transparency early on, and when possible, share whatever you can whenever you can with whomever you can.

For me, some degree of transparency is nonnegotiable. Transparency is one of the reasons I started MacLaurin Group. If you create it, you control it.

TODAY IS THE RAINY DAY

Every founder has a list of things they need to take care of but have not gotten around to yet. We have other priorities. We tend to put out the largest fires first, and leave anything that is only slowly smoldering alone, until we have the resources to focus on putting it out. But you do not want to enter the private equity process with any embers smoldering. First, should one of them flare into a flame, you certainly will not have more time or availability to handle it once you are in the thick of pitching yourself to investors. More important, some of these embers might be fanned by the partnership process itself.

Say you read a complaint on Glassdoor from one of your employees, expressing frustration over a lack of communication. You used to do a good job of sending out monthly updates but that has fallen off this year because you have been busy. You intend to reinstate the updates, but you have not gotten around to it yet.

You must do so in advance of the investment process. If you wait, people will feel you are only doing it because of the process, that it is all a show and therefore disingenuous. Rather than hearing a message of appreciation and respect, your employees will assume you are pretending to be something you are not. When private equity firms come to look at you and you have failed at genuine appreciation of your employees up to this point, I guarantee that is what they will think.

Sometimes, tasks are in the rainy day category because we are specifically avoiding them, especially surrounding personnel. If you are the kind of leader who hates conflict, you must gin up the courage now or risk far more conflict down the line. For example, say you have employees who are not aligned with your vision—is the message you are sending to investors consistent with what they will see? You must resolve current issues or encourage people to move along, especially if the problem person is on your management team. If you do not want someone to have equity following the sale, they cannot be around for the sale.

DEPUTIZE YOUR MANAGEMENT TEAM

Now is the time to lean on your team. It is rare that a business will be better immediately on the other side of a transaction, simply because management team members are distracted by the process. But it does not have to be that way. You don't have to hear yourself saying, "Well, we had a down quarter, but that makes sense because the management team was distracted by the transaction, so no need to worry, we are still doing great as a company." Instead, you can head into your deal stronger than ever. Following these basic rules will make all the difference.

COMPARTMENTALIZE

First, compartmentalize deal meetings. Schedule them separately. Do not let deal conversations bleed into the regularly scheduled meetings you use to run the business. If you allow transaction conversations to enter your regular meetings, they will completely take over. Schedule separate, distinct meanings for all conversations relating to the deal.

SPECIALIZE

We had a client who was able to achieve an incredible amount of productivity *during* their private equity transaction. Their strategy was essentially to divide and conquer. Some management team members were pulled onto the deal team. Others were responsible for keeping the business going. Crucially, the latter group was given clear direction that their duties were equally as important as those of the people working on the transaction.

Not everyone needs to be involved in the transaction equally. If so, everyone's other duties will suffer equally. However, everyone's work does need to be valued equally. Otherwise, those who are not part of the transaction will worry about their roles following the transaction (more on this later).

Then, just make sure you update those team members who are now dedicated to running the business, so they are always engaged and up to speed. First, they must feel included. Second, you never know when you may need to pull them into transaction conversations. Even if that happens at the last minute, they should be well informed so your message to your future partners will never be disjointed. Keeping everyone up to date after meetings is much less of a burden on them than requiring them to be in every meeting.

As for those you do pull onto the deal team, you can spread the burden among them as well. The sheer energy required to stage the same show over and over again—delivering your pitch to the third, fourth, and fifth audience of investors as enthusiastically as you did for the first—is staggering. Having other actors on stage will help keep it fresh. Several of them can play the same part, and you can swap them out from meeting to meeting. That way everyone is taking on some of the weight without needing to attend every meeting and dinner. Then they don't get exhausted either.

Long story short, you do not want anyone in management to feel more or less important. When people get paranoid, they might start jockeying for position, or they might behave in the best interest of their own position rather than of the company. They might become a liability rather than an asset.

DEPUTIZE

Everyone has a role. One of those roles must be that of a First Officer. If you have established with your management team that everything pauses while they wait for you to approve or make decisions, that must change. For the day-to-day business to continue running, even while you are focused on the deal, you will need a number two. Choose one person, one of your chief operating officers, who can act as CEO if you are not available, who will make sure the boat engine doesn't stall or go idle.

Typically, that person is your CFO, but it does not have to be. Whoever it is will be someone comfortable making the tough decisions. There will be times when that person will have to make a decision on your behalf. Further, this person needs to be able to know when it is appropriate to represent you and when they should pull you away from the transaction instead.

Then, do the same thing for each of your biggest responsibilities.

For example, if you are the primary salesperson, make sure someone else on your management team can run point on sales while you are busy seeking investment. You cannot just stop sales for two to three months. If there is absolutely no one else who can handle sales, then you must be very clear with private equity firms. Say, "Look, I am the one and only salesperson. These are the meetings that I have, this is the pipeline, and this is the protected time you can't interrupt because it's revenue that's growing our business." If they are the right partner, they will be amenable to that message.

YOUR ROLE ON THE OTHER SIDE

You now have a management team that is taking on more responsibility and broader responsibility. This is the perfect time to consider how your role might change on the other side of the transaction.

Before the transaction, you and your investors will decide who will be on the board. Sometimes, you will become the Chairman of the Board, and someone new will be the CEO. You would remain a visionary entrepreneur and either you handpick someone internally to become CEO or the private equity firm brings in someone they believe in, who has experience in the area you need for growth and usually who has been a CEO of other portfolio companies. The remaining board seats will typically be held by members of the private equity firm and by their advisors.

This scenario is more common with buyout investors who have majority ownerships. Often in that case, founders know they want to step away from the day-to-day running of the business (or more likely they are asked to step away), but still want to be involved. Especially, if you are rolling part of your investment back into the company post transaction, you will still want to have a voice.

You and your new partner may prefer that you stay on as CEO. This is the most common course of action for growth investors who will have only a minority interest. The founders' leadership qualities, industry expertise, and gravitas are part of what they are buying.

Of course, you will not *solely* be in charge of choosing your new role. Your board, your advisors, and your new bosses will all have a say. Then again, if you have truly chosen the right-fit partner, they will see value in you. Either way, it is important to take a minute to determine what you want. Here are some things to think about.

Has it simply been brutal for you to have to deputize during the transaction process? If you have hated being unable to make all of the day-to-day business decisions, you may want to get back to doing what you love once you are on the other side of the transaction, and stay on as CEO. On the other hand, maybe you will come out of the transaction process with a sense of pride about how much your managers accomplished as a team, and will be charged up about the idea of stepping out of the day-to-day operations in order to focus more on strategy and vision as the chairman of the board. And I will say again that you need to be honest with yourself and ask this tough question: will you wish to work as hard on a Monday after a large deposit is made to your bank account the previous Friday?

Whatever you are thinking, be transparent with your future partner and advisors.

WHAT IS CAP TABLE TRANSPARENCY? (AND WHY YOU WANT IT)

The capitalization table (or cap table) is, among other things, a record of equity ownership in your company. Typically, the table is shared in one of two ways: (1) Either the CEO and CFO are the only ones who know how much equity each member of the management team has; or (2) every participant in the table knows every other participant's percentages. At this point, you will not be surprised to hear that I think whoever put money into the company should be able to see how much money everybody else has put into the company.

As the team is making decisions and different people are pulling their weight, it is good for everyone to know how much skin they each have in the game. For example, if you and I are debating really hard over some part of the transaction deal, and then I realize that 25 percent of the company is at stake for you but only 2 percent is for me, then I'm probably going to let it go. I will offer my advice on the topic, but I will understand that you have way more equity on the line. When everyone knows everything, conversations tend to be more equitable.

After the transaction, everyone on your management team should know they will receive equity after the sale, and they should know how much everyone else is getting. You do not want someone thinking, "I need to be in every meeting so I can be seen and heard to prove I am valuable so I get my part of the pie."

Instead, you want them to think, "I will attend any meeting you need me in, but otherwise, I will make sure we are still on track with our clients."

And if there is someone on your management team who you do not want to have equity afterwards...refer back to the Rainy Day section earlier in this chapter.

Granting equity after a transaction with a private equity firm is one of the most rewarding things you will ever be able to do as a founder of the company. It is real money. You should not give it away lightly. In fact, it should not be given away at all—it should be earned. When you grant someone equity, they get a vote as well as a payout. Your cap table should be a celebration of your team.

If you feel the need to hide it, that suggests you are not willing or not able to defend your equity decisions. You should be able to say, for example, "Everybody is incredibly important. I believe that for the future of this business, the demands I ask of our VP of Sales and of our CFO are a higher degree of demands than what I ask of the rest of you. That is what you will see reflected in their shares."

Whether or not you shared that information, you as a leader will be engaging with your VP of Sales and CFO as if they are more valuable to you...because they are. So why not celebrate your conviction of the reasons with candor? Full transparency allows everyone to respect everyone else's stakes and roles. No one should question whose roles are more valuable to the company or who has put more money into the company. Those should be things everyone on your management team understands.

Finally, when you make the cap table transparent, you are telling your team that you are a leader who makes equity decisions for the right reasons (rather than say, nepotism or favoritism). By doing so, you express that your decisions are defensible, which make your team trust you more and be more likely to reinvest their payout after the transaction.

If, as a founder, you are not distributing ownership to your employees, then all the "Rah! Rah!" around selling will be for naught, since they will not like the fact that you are getting rich and they are not. That is okay if that is the decision that was right for you, but you will need to own it. You might want to consider a private equity partner that has a good track record of incentivizing employees. Employee engagement needs to happen at all levels. If this is important to you, have the conversation with potential partners about their track record for granting vested ownership within their portfolios.

CLOSING THOUGHTS

And what about clients? When you are handling this process effectively, your clients will not even know you are on the market—not because you are hiding it from them, but because you have not slipped up a single bit in delivering your value to them, in making sure they are happy, and in continuing to seek and implement their feedback.

Further, once you are on the other side, you don't want your clients to feel like you flipped a switch on them. Obviously, several things will change. The point is that you need to manage and control how all of that information is relayed to your clients.

Things will change. That is the whole point of getting

investment. One hopes things will change for the good. Either way, you never want the ripples of figuring out who you are as a new company to be felt by your clients. That is why it is so important to draw a precise map, which is what we will discuss in the next chapter. Your clients should deal with the positive results of your changes, not work through those changes with you.

BELIEVE WHAT YOU ARE SELLING

Everyone tries to make themselves look the very best when they are putting themselves up for sale. Yes, you want to give yourself the best chance you can in the market. But do not stretch so far that you are not sure whether or not you can accomplish what you have sold. Some founders get so caught up in putting their best foot forward that they trip over it. If you promise something unachievable, and you do wind up with a private equity partner, what happens next will not be good for either of you.

Ultimately, you will have to be the one following through on your plan. Do not get so caught up in the sales process that you become a salesperson instead of a founder. Your job is to celebrate your true story. You should hardly even need to practice the presentation because it is so genuine and authentic. Lying is much harder than telling the truth.

You know your company and believe in your company. If you did not, you would not be able to sell it. Therefore, there is no reason to try to sell snake oil. Your company is good enough just as it is.

No doubt, it will be an intense couple of months. You will

probably spend a few nights in your office. But if you prepare in advance, spread around some of the work, and are completely transparent about all of it, you can pull it off without disruption.

Are you feeling focused and ready? Then it is time to choose the right Admiral for you and together set your course.

CHAPTER 6

MAPMAKER MAKE ME A MAP

Several people wanted to sail your boat with you. You chose the perfect Admiral. Now what? It is go time.

During the first hundred days of this partnership, you will have an enormous amount to accomplish. First, you will renovate, reinforce, and add onto your boat. Then, you will set sail on a route you and your Admiral devised specifically because your craft and crew can handle it. Finally, you will meanwhile also build a state-of-the-art port to sail in and out of again (and again [and again]).

Arrive well rested. Uncertain seas allow little time for sleep.

WHAT IS A ROADMAP?

The one thing you need before setting off on any voyage, whether by land or by sea, is a map.

In this case, it's a growth plan made specific: budgets,

board members, incentives, execution of technology needs, hiring plans, sales-pipeline plans, milestones, accountability, and on and on, depending on your company's specific needs. You had a rough draft of your roadmap before you even went in for meetings. In other words, you understood your company and yourself well enough to know exactly how you wanted to grow and what you needed to do it. Then, during the due diligence process and any other presale meetings, you, your advisors, and the people who are now your investors all decided on what would be required for you to grow in that way.

The roadmap is a little bit like a hymnal book: everybody has the same copy and knows how to approach each part in unison. You are all singing off the same page. Sometimes this roadmap lives as a PowerPoint presentation. Sometimes it is in a fancy app distributed to all the key players. The point is, it is a plan, you have all agreed on it, and, by the way, it is on a timeline.

In three to five years, your current investors will trade their stake to someone new. The next private equity firm will look at everything you did during these three to five years and assess whether or not it has been foundational for future growth. Will decisions you make today negatively impact that future transaction? The care and attention you put in initially pays huge dividends later.

The first hundred days is the sprint portion of your strategic roadmap. The following three to five years is the marathon. Out of three years, the first hundred days is one-tenth of your total time. And the hundred-day plan begins on day one, not day five or eleven. The first hundred days is not "prep" time. There is only a small amount of time for getting together to get to know each other better and plan more. Why? Because you made sure that already happened throughout the process. Now you have to make good on the growth you promised. Begin executing your operational value creation together immediately.

This is why it is so important that you were completely transparent from the start, and that you honestly assessed what you want and need so that you are set up for success and ready for the speed of this. To have a high internal rate of return, you have to make every minute matter. On the other hand, if you wait until after the sale to reveal potential hurdles or discuss what you will need to achieve growth, you will lose time from the start.

The first hundred days is when your partners will be most present, and when you will all be doing the most heavy lifting. It is also when you set the tone for your employees and culture, for how you are going to engage with this growth. Going back to our boat analogy, you want everyone on your crew to know what their daily role is and also how it plays into the bigger voyage, because this is not a journey you have taken before.

You will not necessarily accomplish everything in the roadmap during the first hundred days, but you will definitely determine how the next three to five years will develop.

In short, there is a lot happening, it is happening all at once, and every single part is incredibly important. No pressure, right? Although the exact roadmap will be different for every company, just as the goals for growth will be different, I can still offer five key pieces of advice: replicate your talents, do not go it alone, prepare for C-Suite additions, communicate transparently, and hire with passion.

Let's take a closer look at each.

REPLICATE YOUR TALENTS

To scale up, you and whatever made you successful so far must be copied and recreated again and again.

Remember in chapter 4 when I told you about Royall & Company's second round of private equity investment, that we specifically sought a private equity firm that would support us in building out a sales team, since Bill was stepping back from sales? That is also something that made us attractive to investors. Investors could easily anticipate how much the company would grow with an expanded team of industry subject matter experts who could emulate Bill. These investors were not making an assumption. There was proof: Bill had already demonstrated that he could be emulated.

Heed this piece of advice in advance of taking your company on the market: No matter how successful you are as a founder, you cannot just expect private equity firms to assume your business will be able to scale up. You have succeeded because of who you are as a founder—as a leader, as a salesperson, as a human. So why would any investor think other people could do your job unless you have a track record of showing exactly that? Are you investing in your team in ways such that they are equipped to emulate you?

Bill met personally with every Royall & Company client. Clients believed in him. Still, even though his gravitas meant he was the one to most often close a deal, he had still built a support system around himself—our management team and senior leaders. If you had spoken to any of us, you might have mistakenly thought we were founders because we believed so strongly in the company's vision and culture. In that way, he had already built the foundation of which the company would grow and scale.

Private equity firms were able to see the huge opportunity of expanding the sales team to emulate Bill and his personal, relationship-based approach. Investors knew that Bill would not put just anybody in front of a client. He had never done so in the past and he remained passionate about what it meant to be client facing. New hires would have to understand the values and goals of the company and be equipped to think through what a right partnership looks like—that would lead to more success—and they needed to be industry subject matter experts.

To be clear, emulation is not cloning. I am not telling you to create a bunch of "mini-mes." Companies are stronger when containing a choir of various voices and notes. But if your choir members are not singing in harmony, it will not be a pretty song.

We see founders all the time who do not know how they do what they do. You must figure this out before you seek private equity partnership. I am not saying that if you have not proved you can be emulated, then you will not get investment. You might. But you will have a much harder time executing your roadmap and scaling your company. And it will take you longer to do so.

Think about what makes you successful as a founder. Why do clients select you? How are you closing deals? If you know the answers to these questions, all you have to ask an investor is, "Can you surround me with support for that?" Further, if you can point to a place in your business where you have already been emulated, then investors will know that the value you deliver is not just in yourself but also in your business.

Tom Formolo, of New Harbor Capital, was a partner with CHS Capital when it acquired Royall & Company during our second round of investment. He recalls being interested specifically because, he says, "It was still 'founder flavored.' Bill was still involved but, most importantly, had a management team of senior leaders who each had founder characteristics yet also distinguished themselves. It was almost like a Royall family."

DO NOT GO IT ALONE

Lean on your advisors. Whomever the private equity firm brought in to support the transition, whether the MacLaurin Group or otherwise, they have done this before. Trust them and utilize them as much as you can as sounding boards. Part of why you are as prepared as you are is because you have been engaging with them from the start. You are no longer the only one in charge, so do not feel the burden as if you are. Hold other people accountable at each step of this journey. And yes, if you and I are partners, I expect that you will hold me accountable.

Your new board will be comprised not only of private equity investors but also additional advisors with pertinent industry experience. Further, your board will likely be made up of successful business leaders who wanted to invest in the fund. They are motivated for your success. Listening to the different perspectives and opinions on your board will provide you with expertise you would not have otherwise had.

I understand that this is a difficult transition both emotionally and in practice. As a founder, you had complete control of your business. You never had to ask permission, you never had to defend decisions. Now, you have a board. That is a different way to run a company. In some ways, it will be difficult to no longer have complete control. But if you lean into their advice and skillsets, and share both the burden of work and the accountability, you will find you can succeed more as a group.

PREPARE FOR C-SUITE ADDITIONS

Your new partner private equity firm will want to weigh in on hiring decisions for any new management team positions. This is often the biggest struggle for founders. Founders consider hiring executive team members as a process near and dear to their hearts. It is your team. It is personal. I think that is why it can be shocking to founders when they no longer have the ultimate decision-making authority over this process.

Rather, I hope having professional opinions will come as a relief. Your new partners have additional understanding of the position for which you are recruiting. They have grown companies like yours before. The firm may want to pull someone from a previous portfolio who really knows the industry or discipline. Or they may want to pull someone from inside your current team. The process may move faster than it has in the past or it may take longer. Simply because I so often see founders surprised by this shift in hiring decisions, I want to spend some time discussing the typical thought processes behind a handful of the most common C-Suite hires.

(A quick side note before we dig in: remember that the role of CEO is also technically a management position being hired. You know you are the right CEO for the next wave. They believe you are as well. But if you get cocky or lazy, they will second-guess their decision. To be blunt, no one is irreplaceable. The private equity firm is buying your company for your story and for who you are—but that does not necessarily mean that is how it will work out. I am not saying it is common for private equity firms to replace founders when that was not part of the plan. I am saying that you need to make sure you do the best job you can because if you do not fulfill the expectations of the role of CEO so that the private equity firm is able to get their return on investment, then you will be replaced, no matter how lovely you are.)

CONTROLLER TURNED CFO

If you have not yet had a proper CFO, but have had someone in more of a controller position, expect your new private equity partner to insert someone into a CFO position. So many of your growth goals will require keeping a keen eye on all of your numbers. Before, you may have thought of this position as task oriented: someone who keeps the light on, keeps budgets and spending on track, conducts year-end processing, and manages similar back-office tasks.

Moving forward, however, you will need a CFO who works alongside the private equity firm to make sure you are growing the business according to plan. This person will be deeply engaged with the strategy side of your decisions and will be a part of all communications surrounding how you utilize your investment dollars and where the return on your investment is coming from. In other words (and especially if your company is small) you may be accustomed to having a controller who basically managed accounting, whereas now you will have a CFO who is a strategic partner in growing your business. You can expect this to be one of the first hires the private equity firm makes.

EXPECT A CHIEF SALES OFFICER AND CHIEF MARKETING OFFICER

Your new private equity partner will likely want to fill these new positions—maybe from your current team and maybe not. Sales teams and marketing teams almost always grow as part of a private equity transaction. Do you have someone who is already experienced leading a sales or marketing organization? Or have your sales and marketing managers simply been winging it and going with their guts, even if successfully?

Just because someone is a really good salesperson does not make them a strong chief executive for sales. Being good at closing deals does not mean they can lead and hold accountable a sales team. The same goes for marketing. Robin Green, President of Ascend Performance, an award-winning Sandler Training company, believes that is one of the biggest mistakes organizations make. "Assuming that your best salesperson would make a great sales manager is one of the 'cardinal sins' organizations commit. It's a completely different skillset. Going from a producer to one who trains, coaches, and supervises can be a significant challenge." Think clearly about what is needed for each of these roles. Know where you can leverage the team you have and where you cannot.

YOU NEED A VISIONARY CTO

This is your chance to get the technology right, once and for all. Likely your technology needed revamping even for your current clients. And now you also need to build it in a way that will scale for growth. But that is not all. You need to build in a way that can be scaled again and again—for when you are up for sale three to five years from now, and again six to ten years from now, and again ad *infinitum*, let's hope. No. Let's do better than hope. Let's hire a visionary CTO and VP of Engineering to get us there.

As a founder—even if you founded a software company—you most likely have a business focus and background which led you to hire a technologist (most often a generalist) to build your software. Most often, whoever builds the original architecture will get bored and want to move on to the next software project. This person is rarely a good CTO who can architect and provide strategic vision. Chances are neither is he or she a good VP of Engineering who needs to manage people, projects, and schedules well.

A good VP of Engineering will put in place processes and structures, keep the trains running on time, and enjoy managing people, conducting annual reviews, and putting together career development plans for the day-to-day management of the team. Conversely, a good CTO will focus efforts on vision and architecture to scale your business for growth. Keeping a good CTO steeped in the day-to-day management of people, projects, and schedules is a waste of their highest value talent and contributions. The most successful CTOs lean on their VP of Engineering for the critical role of managing people, projects, and schedules well. Truly rare is a CTO who is good at all things.

A visionary CTO can scale out in a way that supports existing infrastructure while also being thoughtful of the future. You want future buyers to see where their own roadmaps fit in, and how they can take the company to the next level. You do not want them to have to rebuild. You need a CTO who can position you for future growth, someone who is not just a technologist or a manager, but a true visionary, who is not just answering the question in front of them but making sure you are not being boxed in for the future.

Technology should not be driving your business. Your business drives how the technology supports it. In that way, technology should never be a roadblock or thing that slows down the business's growth. A visionary CTO will not just build the architecture you need now but an architecture that can extend to whatever idea you and your clients imagine for next week, next month, or next year. (We will talk in the next chapter on the importance of keeping technology projects to less than two years.) When you do not have to keep rebuilding it, it is not a roadblock to your growth.

This does not mean your current technologist will no longer have a role in your organization. Even more important than their tech skills is their institutional understanding behind the technology they built. They know why they did what they did. Usually, it was in response to client requests or product requirements.

Most likely your technologist has a lot of pride in the work they have done and is also not accustomed to having a boss critiquing it and poking at it. A visionary CTO will recognize the contributions of your current technologist and will celebrate that person, regardless of whether or not there is a role for your technologist in the organization going forward—all of which will aid in the execution of your roadmap. Again, you want no roadblocks coming from your technology team.

This brings us to my next piece of advice, which may sound familiar...

MANAGE HIRING EXPECTATIONS

These are very tough conversations. Work hard to honor and be respectful of the folks who got you where you are. You also need to honor and be respectful of what the company needs going forward. It is never just a given that the person who is currently sitting in a chair will get to take on the more expanded role of that chair.

Most likely, your current VP of Engineering thinks they will be CTO. They probably will not. There is also the possibility you will not have a place for them going forward. If you want to keep them, make sure they understand why they will not be the CTO, and at the same time why they are hugely valuable in whatever role you want them to fill moving forward. Repeat this process for every personnel change that is coming.

DEVELOP A CLIENT ADVISORY BOARD

One of the best things you can do to ensure a smooth transition is to create a client advisory board. Collect a handful of trusted clients and pull them in close. Share product ideas and strategies with them in advance of implementation and ask them to be completely open and honest with you about their reactions. You will get invaluable feedback and vested buy-in. They get to hear news first and weigh in on ideas. Joan Isaac Mohr described her experience and participation in Royall & Company's advisory board,

"As the line of products and services grew to be the largest share of my budget—somewhere over a million a year—it was still the 'gold standard' in my world. By inviting several of his longtime (and some new) clients to be part of an advisory board to help shape the company, he continued to respect those of us in the hot seat. We felt listened to, while providing or evaluating new ideas and products to grow the company and its revenue."

Choose clients that have a line of sight across all your products and services. Choose the clients who see you as a partner, not as a vendor. Most important, choose those who tell you when you mess up or when they think you have not done a good enough job. Those are the voices you need in a room. Probably you will be choosing clients who are already your references. Just make sure you are not picking those who only ever give positive feedback.

Start with a small group, just a handful. It should be an honor to be invited, and you want to leave room to be able to grow it later, if you need to. I suggest having in-person meetings so they can meet one another and collaborate.

A couple of beautiful things will happen. First, you will get to see how clients react before you implement products or strategies in front of your broader group of clients.

Second, those who are on your panel will become a part of the process—they will be vested and become your advocates. Then, if other existing clients begin to grumble that you are no longer the same company anymore because of your relationship with this new investment firm, your advisory panel advocates will push back. They will spread the word that you are definitely listening to and engaging clients, that your new products and strategies will help existing clients, and that you will be a better company as a result of the investment firm.

And that is important as you grow. The successful scale and growth means you no longer can be in every client meeting. Clients will understand and support you, like Joan Isaac Mohr did: "Of course the staff had expanded considerably, so I worked directly with staff and not as much with Bill. But I knew he was there and he'd take my call in a heartbeat if needed. Plus, he motivated his staff to be as attentive and responsive as he had been."

COMMUNICATE TRANSPARENTLY WITH CLIENTS

I shared a few thoughts about this in the last chapter, but it warrants more discussion. Once your sale becomes public, people will start sharing the information among themselves. Will your clients hear the news from one of your account managers or from the grapevine? Will the news be delivered with excitement and optimism or cynicism and gloom?

You need to control the narrative as much as possible. You know this partnership will be good for your clients, so make sure they know it too. Before your hundred days begins, put a plan in place for how you will communicate the news to your clients, along with any changes they should expect. Determine who on your team will speak with which clients and when and exactly what information should be delivered. I am not saying you need scripts, but you do need to design a very specific, actionable plan.

Every founder will have a different plan, depending on their circumstances. Think about who you will reach out to first. Of course we value all of our clients, but it will be nearly impossible to get ahead of communication if you are making personal phone calls to everyone. Speed of communication is critical. Which clients will you reach out to personally, which ones will your management team contact, and which will hear from your account managers and sales team? Will some receive personal phone calls and some be on an email blast? These are questions to ask yourself. Talk to your deal advisors as well.

And then determine which parts of the news are most important for which clients to hear. What should they expect? Are you staying on as CEO? Is your name changing? Will they be able to get in touch with you in the same way? Most importantly, let them know how this new partnership will benefit them and what they will get out of it. Remind them of your commitment to your products and services. Effective planning will ensure that your clients hear your true message rather than fall prey to rumor-mill fears.

COMMUNICATE COMING CHANGES TO EMPLOYEES

Think about this while choosing your partner as well. A right-fit partner will respect your employees and the need to manage their expectations through communication. However, the anxiety from when people fear their jobs will change is far worse than how their jobs will actually change. It will take you much less effort to communicate in advance than it will to be in reactionary mode after people raise questions or behave in ways driven by fear.

Communicate the momentum and the excitement that come with improvements to be implemented, while at the same time eliminating fears and rumors. Your employees do not know what's in your head. They have not been in all the meetings. If you have hired bright, talented folks who believe in your mission, then you do not want to let them go. You will find a role for them somewhere, because they know your business and are your most valuable asset.

Remember that "RoyFoo" project Jim Milbery discussed in the breakout box in chapter 4? That is a product we developed for internal use at Royall & Company, and one of our growth plans following the first round of investment.

Let me back up. We developed marketing and recruitment tools for colleges and universities. Each product was unique, depending on the school and its needs. We provided a bespoke service. Still, there were certain foundational elements that we knew every single client would benefit from. These were fundamental best practices for marketing and recruitment that every client should have as part of its product's core functionality, regardless of its individual strategic goals. And we had tremendous data and analytics bearing this out.

Further, our creative teams—web designers, copywriters, art directors—had expressed frustration about having to recreate these pieces of core functionality again and again. RoyFoo (I am sorry to keep repeating that name, Bill), was our way to create an internal platform so that every new product began with all these core functionalities already in place. Then, our creative teams came in to design each product for each client's specific and custom needs. This allowed for scale.

When we started explaining the plan, we got a lot of pushback. "You're going to take away my creativity." Or, "You're going to take away my job."

No. The new platform was built specifically to support them. It was a reimagination of the way we had previously routed those manual "green folders" to allow for deeper collaboration and remove from their work those tasks they found uninteresting. They would now spend more time at work focusing on their own high-value contribution for clients.

Even seasoned entrepreneurs will have pushback from their teams during the huge transition catalyzed by investment. If you are not communicating the why behind the what, people will draw their own conclusions. Share the goals of your plan with all your employees and, further, have each manager communicate in more detail with their departments. Also prepare them for a nonlinear path toward growth.

Nasser Chanda, of Paymerang, advises, "It is important to be able to embrace organizational chaos with growth and some ambiguity. Be flexible and accept that there will be change."

How you are structured now is not necessarily how you will be structured in a few months. People will have to take on different roles at different times because of the sheer volume of growth. Your team should understand that there is really hard work involved in a successful transition. And you should understand that if your team members are strong enough to handle it and excited enough about the mission, then you need to fight to keep them onboard, happy, and excited to jump in and do whatever it takes.

Chanda recalls the growth following his private equity investment, saying, "Often, employees thought I was contradicting myself by instituting new structures while asking them to embrace chaos. People asked which one I wanted, and I would say, 'Both.'"

HIRE WITH PASSION

Every month at Royall & Company, we had a company meeting where Bill stood up and introduced new employees. He had them each explain why they chose Royall & Company as well as what school they attended and why. Then he told the story of Royall & Company, our mission, and why he started the company. Every. Single. Time. Somehow, it was always as if he were saying it anew. We never tired of hearing it because we were proud of it and excited about it. We knew it was important that every new employee who came in during a growth period had to buy into the experience and culture.

Part of how I knew Chanda and Paymerang were a right-fit client for MacLaurin Group? He holds the same kind of company meetings. "I worry that people think I'm a broken record," he says. "'Why are you repeating yourself again? We've all heard it!' My response is, first of all, we haven't all heard it. Second, it's very different if I were to say it to a handful of new hires each month, or if I say it to all of us in front of that handful of new hires so that everyone is reminded in that moment of excitement what our culture is and how we are growing our commitments to one another."

By reminding current employees at the same time you explain it to new hires, you pull them into the initiation of the new hires. That is how you grow together. Chanda adds, "If you don't want to keep hearing the story—being part of the culture, helping others come in—then you are probably the wrong person to join Paymerang. Investing in others matters. What if every person who walks through the door gives 5 percent more because they believe deeply in the culture? Imagine that compounded each year for growth."

Paymerang grew from thirty employees to eighty in a single year. It can be tempting, when tasked with growing that quickly, simply to put butts in seats. But now is when it is more important than ever to hire only those people you want to retain—and then work to retain them by giving them accountability in some kind of work ownership. You cannot think about short-term growth. You will not have the bandwidth to deal with the repercussions of losing people or having to replace wrong-fit people. You want these very same employees to be around in three to five years, when you are assessed again.

High-growth companies will inevitably make the wrong hiring decisions. If there is a wrong cultural fit or someone does not align with the values of the company, they could be destructive to the culture. One bad apple spoils the bunch. Employees are watching to see what management will do about it. Remember that a decision not to address the situation is a decision in itself. Your action, or lack thereof, will be reflected in how your leadership is perceived.

CLOSING THOUGHTS: PAUSE, CHEERS

Before you turn the page, take a moment to celebrate. You found a right-fit partner. An investor believes in you and is giving you money and resources. The pitching process is over!

However, rather than being the end, it is literally the

beginning. So do not take more than a moment to celebrate. Everyone is looking to you to have the energy and excitement to carry them all through the first hundred days and the next three to five years. Do not mess up because you were too exhausted by the investment process itself. It is definitely exhausting. But there is no rest for the weary. Now is not the time for you to tone it down. Keep ramping up.

What now? You have fixed your boat, set your route, and know where you will be going. Now you are ready to set sail.

CHAPTER 7

TENDING TO THE SHIP WHILE YOU SAIL

You have shattered champagne on the hull of your boat and set sail. Congratulations! Even though reaching your destination is one of the most important goals you have ever set out to achieve, do not race there as fast as you can. While in route, you must continue to take time to tend to your craft, including making improvements, and stopping at designated checkpoints along the way to check in with your crew, pick up new passengers, and assess the journey. All of this will ultimately ensure you reach your destination faster.

Together, you and your private equity partner will focus on three areas: risk mitigation, cost reduction (or efficiency), and revenue enhancement. Most of the first sixty days is risk mitigation. Meanwhile, the best private equity firms will also immediately look for projects to enhance revenue, so they are not only making money off of cost reduction and efficiency. I will bring up the RoyFoo project again. That was about revenue enhancement—the ability to offer customers more products by having a platform with more features, while also allowing Royall & Company's customer service to improve (efficiency) by automating all of the standardized manual work. Regardless of which of the three kinds of projects you undertake, it will require change.

In this chapter, I will talk about the importance of running toward change, being data-led instead of gut-led, and getting through the Valley of Anguish.

RUNNING TOWARD CHANGE

Change is not easy, especially for a founder who has built a successful company on an existing technology and knows they have a person in house who can respond and fix problems as they occur, no matter how manual or onerous those patches might be. It takes time to realize that some of your customer support pain and suffering will go away after you take the risk to modernize. I see clients who are stuck in webs of special customizations they have made for each of their customers, and even so, they are afraid to change their systems because of the devil they know and all that. But they must. And so must you.

One of the very first opportunities a founder has when partnering with their new private equity investment is to look at modernizing existing back-and-front technology systems. Chances are you may not be using the latest accountancy or payroll software, and since this is in the wheelhouse of private equity firms, they will most likely look for you to migrate to one of their preferred systems. This allows you to not only upgrade under professional guidance, but will make it much easier for you to report numbers to them, and for them to self-serve, accessing financial reporting whenever they like.

More important are the plans you have to grow your business, which require a modernized technology stack. This is not a mystery to you, as during your reverse due diligence, you made an effort to discover all of your technological weaknesses. And, during the roadmap phase, you and your new partner set a plan for how to fix them. Now is the time to implement the changes.

For example, one of the first things we look at for our clients is if they can move to the cloud and shed some of the administration and logistical burdens of maintaining their own hardware. It is not always possible, but if there can be a "lift and shift" to the cloud, then you gain momentum with forward progress without an overly burdened cost, if done correctly. After a "lift and shift" to the cloud, services are more accessible and scalable real-time. That means everything can be done remotely.

Whatever the modernization project, it must be tailored precisely to the plans and needs of the founder and their new partnership. Know that modernization does not have to be a huge, costly project. It can happen in small steps, as long as each step moves you in a forward direction and is a worthwhile step to take. Sometimes, you have to buy a little time—like when you get a flat tire and decide to drive around on your spare, so you can research better tires instead of just taking whatever is available during an emergency—but the worst thing you can do is nothing.

I will spend the rest of the chapter discussing the two other main considerations when tending to your ship. First, you will want to effectively capture any data that will be needed to measure the impact of any changes to the systems and to get a handle on your growth. Secondly, you want to make sure you are positioned with your new technology to adapt and integrate with potential acquisitions.

BE DATA-LED NOT GUT-LED

When a founder is speaking with private equity investors, it is not enough to say, "We're EBITDA negative due to our investment in growth." But rather to be able to say, "We're EBITDA negative due to our investment in growth. However, our unit economics are positive with an LTV (lifetime value per customer) to CAC (customer acquisition cost) ratio over 5X, which is healthy relative to comparable companies in our industry. Therefore, it is justified to invest in our accelerated annual growth rate of 35+ percent. We see an additional two years of this investment plan, given the available market share in our industry, resulting in the need for $6 million of capital for sales and marketing during this period. We expect to be EBITDA-positive in the third year post-investment." That sounds less like an excuse and more like a plan an investor can get behind. (And for context, anything over 3X is generally considered good.)

Anybody who knows Kelley Powell knows that I am very much data-driven. My background is in data and analytics, in knowing that data tells a story. You may not like the story it tells, but data does not lie. And what a blessing that is. Because if you do not like the narrative, you have the ability to change it. You can positively impact the data by having conversations about why the information is what it is, and then pivoting and digging in to achieve the goals you set.

When I asked Tom Formolo, partner at New Harbor Capital, "Why Royall & Company?" he was quick to respond. "The key components were professionalism, a clear return on investment for clients, data-informed decision-making, and that marketing could all be scaled. More importantly, even though this was a second-round investment, Bill was still highly engaged, so it was attractive because a transition out of the founder had not occurred. What did exist was a highly loyal and committed leadership team capable of running the business, alongside the original founder as Chairman of the Board. There was an opportunity for more team-based selling with subject matter experts."

Hear that? A clear return on investment for clients with "data-informed decision-making."

Make data your best friend. Here is how.

KNOW WHAT TO MEASURE

Before you can set your goals, you must decide what success will look like.

You, your new partner, and your shared advisors will determine a strategic plan for value creation. Then you will all determine which KPIs will evaluate that success, as a way to prove out the hypothesis. You cannot accurately know whether you are failing or succeeding if you are checking the wrong metrics. Sales pipeline, client retention (the most important metric in my opinion), new hires, revenue, employee retention, EBITDA, a timeline for building a new piece of technology—although the metrics will differ based on the strategic goals of each specific growth plan, every company scaling up will typically track five to ten at once.

Choose the metrics that are most important to success. When I spoke with CoolSys CEO and author Adam Coffey, he recalled hearing Jack Welch speak on this topic once, saying, "What gets measured gets done." Coffey adds, "By human nature, we tend to make sure those things we are measured upon are done well." Why not use human nature to your benefit?

Chances are, you will not be on target for all of them all of the time. But you need to know if you are falling too far behind on any of these important metrics at any given time. For example, if you said, "This is what it will take to get to point B from point A, and these are the stops along the way," but then you are a little late getting to the first stop, and a little late getting to the second, you have to ask yourself a series of questions. First, do you have time to recover? Second, what is going wrong?

Let's say we all thought we would be doubling the number of sales we have, but we are not. Do we not have the right sales team in place? Or maybe there is a communication issue. Is there a new competitor in our market? Perhaps the problem is technology. Or maybe our sales team is simply thinking, "We don't believe we can handle this amount of growth, because we're already backed up, so maybe we just won't sell as hard as we should." Whatever it is, we can check the metric, have a conversation around it, and figure out the cause.

A misstep will not just set itself right.

When you track your metrics fanatically, you keep small problems from becoming big problems. With practice, you will let the data get ahead of the problems. Knowing what success looks like for you usually boils down to knowing what success looks like for your clients. That means you need to have in place both what success looks like for each individual client compared to their own goals, and what success looks like compared to the industry.

Jim Headley, Chief Information Officer at MacLaurin Group, advises our clients on building a culture of data analytics. You are not a data-driven business simply because you have a data warehouse, data mart, or team of analysts. By Headley's measure of an analytic culture, "It occurs only when those with a passion and understanding of data context empower those who drive the business through consumable, self-guided analytic discovery." In other words, it is like your story as a founder. Having an analytic culture is not something you do, it becomes part of who you are.

As a founder engaging with a private equity firm, you have made commitments to one another, just as you would to a client. If a client called to say they were unhappy and asked for their money back, would you not say, "If that's what you want, OK—but first, can we try to get it right?" In the same way, if you are not meeting a goal you forecasted on your roadmap, you cannot just throw your hands up in the air and say, "Sorry." You cannot just lower the numbers. You must find a way to pivot and make things right.

THE STORY IS ONLY AS GOOD AS THE DATA YOU COLLECT

When you quantify data, you have to make sure all of your inputs are there. Otherwise, you are not getting the full story, the real story. Say you have a client complaining about a certain aspect of your product. If you only listen to the loudest voice, you could be biased about what is truly happening. On the other hand, if you have accurate data on all client responses, you might determine instead that the complaining client is merely having a training issue, or maybe is upset about something they want but do not necessarily need. Whenever you are making an assertion about what you believe to be true, you need to be able to back it up with data. To that end, ensure that your systems and processes are capturing all of the data you need. As the price of data storage has plummeted, so too have the barriers to data retention. Keep it all, even if you are not sure of its immediate value.

Even the small stuff can matter a great deal. If you are capturing only successful login attempts, your data is biased toward people being successful. If you instead capture every single login attempt, whether the person succeeds or fails, you will have a better idea of how people engage with your system. The story behind your data will be biased by the way you capture it.

The thing about missing data, though, is that you will not know it is missing. It is not that people maliciously hide data (although it does happen, you may think you have a really high close rate because someone is deleting those prospects in the pipeline who said, "no thank you"). But let's say someone closes a deal so quickly that they forget to go back to key into the system all the reasons why the deal closed as quickly as it did. As a result, you do not know which salesperson excelled or the context in which their approach worked. Perhaps you have one salesperson who is really good at tracking everything and three who are not. Your data will be skewed. Without data to understand what actions are successful, it is difficult for others to emulate that same success. Your story will be wrong.

Work with an advisor who has experience capturing all data, not just a few pieces. Challenge your data, challenge what the reports are telling you if something feels off from your instinct. One of two things will happen: You will either discover the data is right and you need to make a decision, or that your data capture is not extensive enough. Either way, it is a win because you emerge with more knowledge.

Once you modernize your technology, it will be a lot cheaper to store and maintain data, so you can capture much more of it and, in turn, learn more about your customers' behavior.

SPREAD THE ACCOUNTABILITY

Paymerang was able to grow from thirty to eighty employees in one year because Chanda was adamant about setting and following metrics. "Metrics must be visual to those who own them and manage them," he says. "I am unwilling to hide or sacrifice unflattering numbers to appease someone's feelings."

That is a really hard thing to do, because you may have a manager or director who has been part of your team for a really long time. But the problem is not their feelings. The problem is where the metric is. So fix it. And you are not going to do that by keeping it private or hiding it as a secret.

Chanda put Paymerang's key metrics, including number of payments processed and number of calls taken in, on display in the office. "Everyone in the company needs to own something. Our CFO supports commercial contract negotiations. Our COO owns risk. Our HR Director was responsible for founding our inside sales team," he adds. Chanda owned Sales because he believes strongly that any CEO in an early stage should not give up Sales or Product, and instead should keep them as long as possible. This way, he continued to have a direct line to the voice of the customer. But he also spread the motivation that comes with accountability.

Doing so means you can also spread around the kudos. The happy reason to communicate your milestones internally is because they provide you opportunities to celebrate with your employees. You told them beforehand what you wanted to achieve with this investment. Remind them why you are all working so hard. It is easy to get busy and just keep pushing forward. But remember that your employees are doing the exact same thing, and if they do not see the fruits of their labor, they will burn out.

I am a celebration person. I think every company should

have a chief cheerleader as one of their employees. Often times that is you as the CEO. You cannot let the developments that you are excited about—new features and functionality, new products and services—be stories you only tell clients. Your employees should be the first to learn of new developments. Keep them informed. Allow them to celebrate. That way you ensure all your clients are hearing the good news.

THE CLOCK IS NOW TICKING

Your goal is to grow the company in the way it needs to grow—for scale. You must also keep in mind that you are now in a predetermined cycle that is ultimately preparing you for the next sale, most likely to another private equity firm. For most founder-led companies, that cycle is three to five years long. At the time of the next transaction, you want your company not only to appear strong, you want to be as strong as possible. You want all data to reveal and support successful growth achieved and ahead. That is a bit more difficult if one of your key modernization projects is still in the middle of being developed.

Even if the project is completed, you must also be able to prove the benefit of it. You need to allow time to execute the build-out, for customers to adopt it, and then for it to grow from there so you can prove scale. You need to demonstrate the value of what has been proven to gain interest and excitement for what's possible ahead. It is a good rule of thumb to keep projects to two years. This does not mean you will never tackle large, impactful endeavors within the private equity space. This simply means you must be judicious in how your roadmap addresses these needs by breaking them down into consumable pieces.

Remember, when planning, that technology projects have a bad reputation for running over budget and exceeding the time frame. Some colleagues take the estimate and double it. I usually take the estimate and add 20 percent (I call this my "what we do not know yet" tax and others fondly refer to it as a "management tax"). We are both right on budget and time frame, some of the time. Although people tend to blame the development and engineering teams for these delays, in my experience, delays are usually due to the business itself not truly understanding what it needs or not being prepared for the logistics of the project.

You may be thinking, *Of course Kelley would say that—she is part of the advisory team providing these technology services.* But in reality, I offer that opinion from my personal experience on the business side of the table. I have before agreed to an estimate without fully understanding the project, and then I wound up making changes to it later. And I have certainly found myself getting excited about what an engineering team is doing for customers and then wound up asking for additional services along the way.

Business representatives must have a seat at the table. The technology team cannot be the only ones developing the technology. Timelines do not typically change. But when you twist them or add things to them, they do expand. Always budget in extra. Always.

DO NOT WAIT TO BE ASKED FOR DATA

One thing founder CEOs have to adjust to is the fact that now they are being regularly asked for information that otherwise they would gather at their leisure. Previously, they were the only ones interested in the information. CEOs who are unaccustomed to being asked a lot of questions might now feel like they have too much oversight and wind up feeling frustrated. It will be easier for everyone if founder CEOs proactively provide the information rather than waiting to be asked.

Even so, as a CEO, you should be prepared at anytime, on any day to show your metrics. Be ready anytime that anybody might ask you for them. After the intensity of the first hundred days, meetings and updates typically happen monthly or quarterly, but you never know when somebody might want to check in. I also suggest sending over your metrics in advance of any meeting. That way you can spend more time in the meeting looking forward. Even better, with the right business intelligence setup, you can have dashboards always available, always updated, for everyone to view and without anyone having to run a report.

THERE TO SUPPORT

If you are not meeting your metrics, your private equity firm is not going to just hang you out to dry. They literally have a vested interest. To be clear, you do not meet metrics, you meet goals. That is an important distinction Jim Headley calls me out on every time. Be sure your metrics demonstrate that you are meeting your goals. When your metrics alert you that you are falling short of meeting your goals, lean on your advisors.

No one is going to know your business as well as you, but your advisors can certainly work with you to figure out why you are not meeting your goals and then pivot so you can. They have experts in different areas, who can come assist you. Welcome the support. You will thank me for that advice. I never would have been exposed to a wider network of world-class specialists whom I now call friends, if it had not been for my private equity relationships.

Again, you must embrace transparency. Explain your struggle and the why behind it. You will not have time to recover if you do not. Remember, the clock is ticking. And, if you fail to share unflattering metrics because you are afraid you will lose your job, then that may become a self-fulfilling prophecy.

And what about when you consistently are not meeting your numbers? Say you are taking your current product into a new industry but it is not generating revenue. Maybe it is taking a loss. You do not want to make the wrong decision by giving up too soon—maybe it just needs more time to get to market. But you also do not want to risk losing your business because you had too much hubris to listen to the market and your clients when they say that you are just not meeting a need. You need to know, in advance, what your "I'm going to call it number" is. Decide early on, because you cannot make that decision properly in the heat of the moment.

MEASURE FROM THE START

Rob Healy, a partner at L Squared Capital, considers meeting financial goals and objectives to be one of the two most important things you can do as a founder looking for future private equity partnership (along with hiring and retaining high-quality people). "Most run into financial pitfalls and then give up. They simply reforecast," Healy says. "What's exciting is the founder who is willing not to give up and instead asks, 'How can we achieve our goals anyway?'"

Healy advises to stay positive and shoot aggressively, while also being realistic. Some founders are more conservative than others. What is important is that your style aligns with your partner's. You and your partner will know if you are aligned based on your history of setting and meeting financial goals and objectives. "It's not always about EBITDA," he says. "You need to align with the why of our goals and what we wish to accomplish together. It's important to be a founder who has shown a capability to make those decisions and choices wisely."

SEAMLESSLY ADD ON ACQUISITIONS

Back when you put together the Confidential Information Memorandum on your company, and first met with private equity firms, you probably identified other acquisition targets that would benefit your company. Perhaps there is a company that has a feature or product that will enhance your service and acquiring the company will get you there faster than building it yourself or through organic growth—one you can completely absorb into your company (what is called a "tuck-in" or "bolt-on" acquisition), or maybe you want their clients. Perhaps the company would continue to exist but under your umbrella (what is called an "add-on" acquisition) as it aligns nicely with your core competencies and can quickly integrate into a new division if not an existing division. In the world of private equity, additional acquisitions are the most common strategy to quickly grow companies following initial investment.

An advantage to partnering with private equity is that they will have a line of sight into potential acquisitions you could not otherwise know about. Potential investment opportunities are constantly being put in front of them. Once you have partnered with them, you become part of a pipeline process that benefits you.

FROM THE OTHER SIDE OF THE TABLE

Acquisitions take time. Remember all of the time and energy you put into selling your business? It was not insignificant, but the good news is you now have personal experience with the process and a private equity team in the boat with you who do this all the time. They will do most of the heavy lifting so you can concentrate on the strategic decision with your partners. What questions do you ask the owners of potential acquisitions to determine whether or not they are a right-fit partner for your business and its growth plans?

The biggest thing that can make or break a partnership is not whether or not your technologies are compatible (more on that to come), but whether or not your cultures are. Have those hard conversations early.

It is not uncommon for a company to be purchased by a private equity firm and then turn around and try to purchase its competitor. Sometimes these deals fall through.

During the process, be as candid as possible while still keeping important business details close to your chest. Even though you all agree you will destroy all confidential information shared during the process of figuring each other out, we are all humans, and once you know a thing, you cannot unknow it.

LESS IS BETTER

Following an acquisition, you must decide which technology system or combination of system parts will ultimately survive. Just because you acquire a company does not mean they should adopt your systems. There will be some things you do better and some things the company you have just acquired does better. Sometimes you might acquire a company specifically because of its technology.

Decide which system will go away and which should remain if there is overlap, because the less infrastructure you have to run, the better. That will save you money and reduce the time getting services to your clients.

If you decide to keep multiple systems, whether short term or for a longer duration, you will want your systems to speak so you can capture complete data moving forward. This is the only way to ensure you see the whole, unbiased story. When you have the complete historical view data at your fingertips, you can make better decisions. Sometimes the easiest path here is not to try to shoehorn data into one system or the other, but to create a brand new data repository and have all systems pour into that, which is a common-use case for a data warehouse.

For example, imagine both companies share a handful of the same clients. These clients especially will need to know who you are as a company now. They should never get two separate phone calls from two different account managers asking them to work with you in two different ways. When you have ensured you see the whole, unbiased story, you can look at every shared customer and determine which company has a better relationship with them, and therefore which primary account manager should be responsible for them.

RETURN TO THE VALLEY OF ANGUISH

As the old adage goes, the measure of a relationship is taken not when things are going well, but when things are going wrong. In this world of private equity, it will not all be smooth sailing, and there will be rough waters to navigate.

In chapter 4, Jim Milbery introduced you to the notion of the "Valley of Anguish," the point in any project where going forward feels equally as painful as it would be to go back. You know that point, where you wonder if the time, money, and resources spent on this project are worth it. You start to challenge all of the original conditions that set this project off in the first place. You question whether the pain that led you to this undertaking was really that unbearable after all.

Since you are most likely reading this as a founder or entrepreneur, let's talk about the Valley of Anguish in regard to your technology modernization project. At the start of every project or modernization of architecture or infrastructure, people are very excited about the change. Then, just when the project is nearly completed, people get project fatigue. They start to forget what is being accomplished and only focus on the negative: the new system will be buggy initially, for example, plus, testing a new system will add onto everyone's existing workload. People will feel exhausted and frustrated and will want to throw everything away.

I am here to tell you that this always happens. When you face this challenge, you will not be unique. In that way, you can be prepared for it and push through. That can be hard, especially if people get a little finger pointy. But if you can recognize that the Valley of Anguish is a healthy part of the process, you can fight the instinct to give up. The really good news about your private equity partner is that they have experienced it and will anticipate it too. They will push you to finish what you started to ensure the business will reap the reward. You cannot fire your private equity investor. And yes, that is really good news. It may be the very motivation you need.

The Valley of Anguish will be experienced most strongly by the business's leaders, who grow anxious and nervous when progress slows. As all good project managers will tell you, 80 percent of any project is typically completed in 20 percent of the time, while the last 20 percent of the project takes ages. I have lived through this pain in many projects with many different portfolios. The underlying reason is usually the same: lack of appreciation for just how complicated and impoverished their existing systems were.

Typically, founders hit the "Valley" when it is time to migrate data from one system into another. Do not rush the process. Make sure you are communicating with the first clients you plan to migrate to the new platform. Phase clients by prioritizing those who will appreciate the benefit of the new technology and are at the very least open to vetting the functionality of the new system together. In a perfect world, you will have clients who are excited at the opportunity to be your first clients on the new platform, and you will navigate those unchartered waters together. You will not be in a position to promise the first clients on the platform that there will be all smooth sailing, but you will be in a position to be in the boat together and immediately react to any rough waters.

Think about when you first started your business. Remember how important it was to choose your first clients wisely? Remember when Mohr said, "Your first clients know your faults, warts and all, so if they stay with you, they will be the most loyal clients you will ever have?" Well now that you are moving your business to a new platform, you will need those same loyal clients to be first on the new platform. Not only will they be the first to benefit from the new technology, they will have patience with you as they pressure test the system. I see the scenario play out too often where founders want to put a fragile client onto the new platform first, as a way to save the relationship. Do not make that same mistake with your modernization project. You need a trusted client to be honest with you on whether the new platform solves their pain points or creates new ones.

TOSS THE ANCHOR IF NEEDED

Private equity will at varying degrees get involved in the daily operations of a company. That said, they are more interested in the larger strategic vision and in making sure everyone remains aligned and continues to move forward. Therefore, and as I have already said, it is vitally important that you all agree what that strategic vision is before you enter the partnership.

Remember you are no longer the lone captain of your own ship. Instead, you are now part of a whole fleet, all working together to move everyone forward. You no longer get to make all the decisions. Where founders often fail and get disenchanted with the world of private equity is when they believe nothing will change and they ignore their new partners.

A word of caution: If all you see are dollar signs, and you believe you can ignore your partners and chart a different course, you will fail. The failure will be miserable, costly, and could potentially destroy your legacy.

With all that said, things can change, including the market. Course corrections are part of any journey and are to be expected. So when a course change is being discussed and you feel it is not in the right direction, then you must present your case. Better to throw the anchor in the water now, to slow down the journey, than to find later that you have sailed in the wrong direction or worse, onto a rock.

The first thing to ask yourself, "Is this change still in line with the original strategic vision?" If it is, then we are now merely discussing execution (as opposed to a fundamental change to the original goal). If the goal has changed, then you have to subjectively look at the data and see if that points to the same conclusion. It is important for all to share information and engage in conversations from the same set of analysis.

Here is the good news: I have never seen private equity make an emotional decision. They make informed decisions. Private equity firms are representing their fund, and to that end, they must justify their decisions to a whole lot more people than just themselves.

Does this mean private equity firms get it right all the time? No. They rely on experts and industry insiders, like yourself, to make sure they make the best possible decision based on the information at the time. On the other hand, data-led processes may be less familiar to you if you are someone who has traditionally followed gut instincts. It is important that you embrace data-led decision-making.

That said, do not let go of that gut instinct. Instead, allow yourself the gift of your gut instinct to be both supported by and augmented with data.

Now, let's assume the strategy is indeed changing, and you are fundamentally opposed to it and cannot execute it in good faith. This may be the time for you to seek a lesser role and let others take it forward. There is no shame or failure in this path. The key is to step down in a way that lets others continue to sail on with relationships maintained. (Your expertise will still be required, so do not feel you are no longer a part of the overall journey.)

Have I seen it all go wrong? I have. But it is rare. You want to avoid being the founder who continues forward, actively undermining the partners. There are unfortunately founders who steer the ship away from doing as the Board recommends, and may even set things up to fail just to prove a point because they feel they know best. This path is a collision course, where you will force your partners to actively remove you for the sake of the company, the employees, and the fund as a whole. This course serves no one. And never think you are so critical to the mission as to give the private equity firm an ultimatum.

On the other hand, if the strategy is not changing and your opinions differ only on the decisions surrounding execution, ask yourself if it really matters, or if it is just a sweet tea versus lemonade situation. You may prefer one over the other but would probably not turn down a chilled glass on a hot day of sailing.

CLOSING THOUGHTS

Above everything, a private equity company is not there to destroy you or tear down your company. Growth and prosperity are the keys to a successful outcome.

There must first be a plan to create value. If the strategy is not working, execution decisions can always be changed. Communication is the key here. You should always feel you can talk with your private equity partner. Remember, the private equity investors are interested in investments where the founder—you—wants to stay significantly involved in the business and wants to grow to the next level but is not sure how. They want to listen.

The skies are clear, the wind is high, and when you look back, you no longer see shore. You did it. Now it is time to turn around so you can do it again.

CHAPTER 8

ONCE MORE AROUND THE CAPE

In three to five years, after you have met your growth plans, your business will be up for sale again. Even though you will have been through it all before, the next round will not be the same. Some of the logistics may be easier, thanks to familiarity, but on the whole, the next voyage will be no less hard.

You will sail around the same Cape, but its physical features will have changed. A sandbar may have formed in what was previously a channel. A hotel may have built a large leisure pier where you previously docked. This time around, you will utilize new and different skills.

Some of you may be wondering why you need to think about this now. It is because growing and scaling a business will keep you so focused that you will blink, and it will be five years later. You have to think about it now. At the same time, this is a book about finding the right-fit partner, not navigating later rounds, so I will keep this chapter brief.

My most important advice: remember your long game when choosing a private equity partner. From the very start, ask them how they imagine their eventual exit. In other words, when they say, "We have done what we set out to do together to grow this company, and now it's time for a new admiral to take over the fleet," what will that mean for you? Will they sell you to someone who will also want you to scale up and stay on as a leader (and then want to sell you again in another five years)? Will they sell you to a strategic buyer who will keep your company distinct but hold onto it forever? Or will they sell you to a competitor who will swallow or dissolve your business?

To be clear, they may not know the answers to those questions yet, but they can tell you their thoughts, and you can look at their track records. Chances are, if a private equity firm is selling to another private equity firm, then they want the CEO to stay. Conversely, if a private equity firm is selling to a strategic buyer, the CEO will be let go, most likely after a transition period.

In the same way that a good strong technology partner will build out new technology systems based not only on what the business needs now, but also what it may need in three to five years (and in six to ten years, etc.), you also need to think about your long-term goals and what your success criteria will be down the road. Similarly, if you think you will want to step away following the next sale, then you and your partner should start grooming replacement candidates right away. Whatever your long-term goals are, they should enter into your original decision-making process.

Here are a few things to think about: You might continue

within another private equity cycle with additional investment to continue to grow your vision; you might undergo
a merger and become a part of someone else's story and
vision; you might be acquired by a current competitor or
someone who wants to be your competitor; or you just
might decide it is time to walk away.

KEEP GROWING

You have grown and new investors want to grow you even
more. This would be very similar to what happened the
first time around. If this is what you and your partner
want for the future of your company, there are things to
plan for now. Throughout the first three to five years and
especially during your follow-up transaction, it is important to keep your leadership team and business "founder
flavored"—a term you heard Tom Formolo use in chapter
6. This is important if your next round is with another
private equity firm or private investors.

For example, we have worked with DolEx Dollar Express,
Inc.'s CEO, Mario Trujillo, in two separate investment
cycles, meaning we advised him as he prepared to go once
more around the Cape. In a subsequent round of investment, Trujillo wanted a right-fit partner(s) who would
distribute equity across his management team and senior
leaders, which ultimately meant less equity for himself.
Much like Bill Royall did, Trujillo planned to spread the
wealth. It is a strong way of saying you care about ongoing
continuity of the business.

Decisions like that speak to a leader's character. Trujillo
could have stepped away, retired and let everyone else take

it from here. Like Bill, Trujillo wanted to see the company continue to grow. He took no credit, and even in our conversation before submitting my final manuscript for print, what was most important to Trujillo was to recognize his team. It is that genuine humility that is the very reason I asked him to allow me the gift of highlighting him as someone founders should emulate. And he is right. The team at DolEx is incredible. They believe in the noble mission and the culture. Trujillo lives his actions as a servant leader every day. DolEx is a financial services company—providing global, electronic, funds-transfer services—but if you ask Trujillo what he does, he talks about relationships and connecting people across the globe so they can support their families with food on the table or mothers having a special gift on Mother's Day. You can bet his management team defines the business in the same way.

Trujillo knows he will eventually be stepping back. He also knows the very best thing you as a leader can do for the future growth of your company may very well be to allow others to lead. Those who have been the reason for the success and growth alongside you will be well mentored for their next sail.

BECOME A PART OF SOMETHING BIGGER

The next wave may have your company being absorbed into or merged with another company, which would be a little different from "business as normal" post transaction. The process of the transaction is not dissimilar, just the end result is. It is less like a round of investment and more like a purchase. In this case, the private equity firm or private investors are not giving you money to scale your vision.

Even though the word is merger, know that there is always a dominant player. Rare is there a true partnership; there is always going to be someone who has the edge. For example, consider the amount of companies that have Co-CEOs? Struggling to name one, aren't you? They exist, albeit few and far between. So assume there is going to be one CEO upon transaction, who will be the CEO? If there are cultural conflicts, who will win? Start preparing yourself now for these conversations—and for either potential outcome.

Culture clash is the most common reason why a founder exits a company prematurely. Avoid that by understanding that culture shifts are evolutionary, not revolutionary. If you and the other company are not in complete alignment, you cannot expect either to adopt the other's culture right away. The earlier you consider various scenarios, and the more you talk to your right-fit partner about them, the better prepared you will be to weather any storm.

As a part of my volunteer service on the da Vinci Angel Advisory Board for VCU, I have the fortunate experience to serve alongside Ting Xu, Founder and Chairman of the Board of Evergreen Enterprises. The company was founded in 1993, when Xu launched a second career for her retired parents making decorative flags in her garage. The company is now one of the nation's largest flag wholesalers, producing millions of flags each year. Xu has grown her business through an acquisition strategy to supplement Evergreen's organic growth.

I spoke with Xu when writing this book, because first and foremost, she is an incredible founder and leader who embodies the true spirit of entrepreneurship in keeping with the values I admire. Secondly, she is an entrepreneur who has a proven growth strategy much like that of a private equity firm. She often competes with private equity when looking at potential acquisition targets. Her passions for product development and creation are embedded in Evergreen's DNA. Evergreen has a proven track record of consistent and timely introduction of hundreds of new products to the market each year for over twenty-five years. When I asked Xu for her advice for founders on what she looks for in an acquisition target, she said, "Founders should implant their passions on their organizations. You cannot be good at or do everything, so finding the right partners, whether internal or external, that compliment your talents is critical." Finding the right partners...sounds like solid advice.

Xu has acquired eight other businesses, oftentimes competing against private equity groups in the process. You might ask yourself how a founder achieves success with eight acquisitions. Remember when I suggested you will want to engage an advisor, an investment banker to help you find potential acquisitions? Remember when I said you want to expand your team with the right hires? Xu believes so strongly in her growth strategy through acquisitions within the middle market and private equity landscape, she hired an investment banker from Harris Williams and Co. with merger & acquisition and private capital advisory services experience to serve on her leadership team.

Admittedly, Xu is somewhat unique. She is somewhere between private investments and strategic buyers. I think it comes down to her ability to see the growth potential in a founder much like that of a private equity company and what she demonstrates in living her own leadership values and story for her company. To Xu, "building a business has never been about the exit, it is about the journey—both my company's and my own. In every deal I look for hidden value that the target's founder or leaders have been unable to unlock. When passionate leaders humbly recognize the limitations keeping their business from reaching the next level, but clearly articulate their future vision, that is when I get super excited about a partnership."

There is a whole separate book that can be written charting the path Xu and others of her drive have taken to inhabit that world where you do not rely on a private equity firm to make the buying and selling decisions. Those are done in-house, if you will, with your own internal "private equity" support team.

CONSIDER A DIFFERENT STRATEGY

Although it is possible for a strategic buyer to acquire you from the start, small to midsize founder-led companies may find they will partner with private equity first, and then sail on with a strategic buyer later. Further, often-times strategic buyers can come out of left field. When Amazon bought Whole Foods, many were surprised by the pairing. In Forbes, Brittain Ladd expressed befuddle-ment, noting that Amazon "plans in terms of a decade?" At first glance, you may wonder why they have an interest in you because the alignment just does not jump out at you. Chances are, they have a growth strategy and your company is how they achieve a jump-start on that growth.

Others are more obvious such as when you fit within their strategy because they were a competitor. One of my most favorite examples to describe a strategic acquisition is the purchase of Nolij Corporation by Lexmark International for $32 million. I was on the management team at Nolij (although I had left by the time of transaction), and I remember how competitive the two companies were. Nolij was a prominent provider of Web-based imaging, document management, and workflow solutions for the higher education market. Lexmark was the leading provider of process and content management software at the time of the acquisition. Our respective teams ran into each other at every trade show and competitive RFP process. I remember John Collins, the president of Nolij Corporation keeping a scoreboard in the office the year we won a crazy wild streak of competitive bids. Lexmark noticed and acquired its competition.

Rather than looking for an Internal Rate of Return on the kind of short-term growth that happens in three to five years, strategic buyers play a much longer game for growth, like Xu at Evergreen.

If your private equity partners sell you to a strategic buyer, then you are no longer in charge of your own destiny. The company you built will now effectively become a department in a larger organization, and you may never be sold as a separate entity again. Depending on the financial arrangement, you may come to the end of your upside cycle when a private equity firm sells you to a strategic buyer. Most likely you will only be there to help in the transition, and they will not wish you to stay. On more than one occasion, I have seen a CEO make a decision to walk away prior to the agreed upon transition timeline, because the commitment they honored no longer made sense. If you are strongly opposed to any of those outcomes, only partner with a private equity firm that agrees with you. Later, you will no longer have a say.

WHEN TO STEP AWAY

It is okay to step away if that feels right for you. Remember, this is about right fit and timing. Some founders know before they ever partner with private equity that they will leave during the second transaction. Some founders have hopes for the second transaction that do not pan out, and wind up exiting as a result. Walking away from your company is not the end of your career. When it feels right to step away, it is the NEXT step in your career.

How do you know it is the right time to walk away? There are signals to begin looking for to know it is time to ask yourself the question. A question only you can answer. What are those signals? You may find you are no longer contributing as much; you may find your value is no longer required; or you may find you are just not as excited to get into the office every day. Do not make a decision over one data point. Everyone can have a bad day. If you find any of this resonates over an extended period of time, then start thinking about stepping away.

Some have the option to stay for another round and choose to become an investor, an advisor, an operating partner for other ventures, or maybe even start their own private equity fund. Maybe you exit to start a new business that fills a niche you recently discovered. Even without any plans, if the second (or third or fourth) transaction does not feel right, it is okay to step away. And sometimes, the growth of the company may very well be better positioned for growth because you did. If you have done it well, your team is ready to step up for their next "once more around the Cape."

Q AND A: ENGAGING WITH LEGAL COUNSEL

If you go around (and around) the Cape, it is even more important to develop a lasting and trusting relationship with your company's legal counsel. Tom Bowden, of Timeless Counsel, PLC, is uniquely qualified to provide founders with advice about this kind of engagement—because he has been a founder himself.

What is your personal experience as a founder and entrepreneur, and with private equity?

Although most of my professional life has been as an attorney representing founders and investors, I had the opportunity to co-found a technology company in the 90s called Integrity Communications with the goal of marketing an end-to-end broadband cable communication system. In 1999, we pivoted into wireless and merged with another company that had complementary technology to form Spike Broadband Systems, which garnered a $400 million, five-year contract in partnership with Siemens AG. At the time this was the largest commercial rollout of non-mobile wireless broadband in the world.

Over the course of more than seven years, my role evolved from general counsel to chief operating officer to director of corporate development for the merged company. Despite that dramatic initial success, Spike did not survive the after-effects of 9/11. Following the bankruptcy, I returned to practicing law in Richmond. In 2012 I launched my own law practice, now under the name Timeless Counsel, PLC. During my legal career, I've had the opportunity to be a provider, consumer, and observer of legal services in the fields of private equity, venture capital, and mergers & acquisitions. I've represented founders and investors, and I've started companies and seen them through all phases of development from pre-organization through liquidity events. All of my experience as a lawyer has been in small to midsize firms (never more than 100 lawyers).

If a founder is thinking about private equity, what is most important to look for in legal counsel to help them through the process?

Without question, the most important thing is a sense of confidence, not only in their technical competence but in their understanding of and alignment with the founder's goals and concerns. The best results come when that alignment is strongest. That's why I do not track my time or charge based on hourly rates. When lawyers, especially in large firms, charge for their time, it is inevitable that their goals will drift out of alignment with those of their clients. A true professional knows the value of their services and should be prepared to agree to a price that shares that value fairly with the client.

What is the one roadblock founders could avoid?

The question of sharing ownership—and by extension, responsibility—for the company's direction. There are so many creative ways to share ownership with investors, co-founders, employees, and advisors that it boggles the mind. All too often, founders think one-dimensionally about majorities and control. Unfortunately, the same independent streak that drives an entrepreneur to found a company, with all the risk and effort that it entails, often leads them astray when they tell themselves that they must preserve some arbitrary level of control or ownership to insure the success of the enterprise and its original goal. Sometimes, companies become great because they pivot and adapt. Nokia's origins can be traced back to Suomen Gummitehdas Oy (Finnish Rubber Works), a manufacturer of galoshes and other rubber products founded in the nineteenth century! Single-minded attachment to the original concept of the founder can be appropriate in the early stages, but may lead to stagnation and ultimate failure if the world changes, as it always will.

If there was something a founder could do to make your role in supporting them easier as they take on an investment, what would it be?

Be totally open. Share their goals, apprehensions, fears and weaknesses. Like a patient who does not tell their doctor about all of their symptoms, an entrepreneur who is not open with their closest advisers cannot expect them to read their mind and render the best advice. If the founder does not trust their adviser enough to share everything with them, they should find another lawyer. This is even more important than technical competence in any specific legal field. Experts are everywhere, and a good lawyer will tap their expertise when needed, especially if the founder's trust in the adviser is based on more than technical expertise. A wise attorney will not try to "protect" the relationship by doing everything themselves, and a wise founder will assure the attorney that they will not be cast aside just because they are not expert in every conceivable aspect of law.

CLOSING THOUGHTS

A quick summary of this chapter: know what you want, understand your business's needs, and be honest and transparent with all players throughout. All right, that was a little joke because that sentence could also summarize pretty much any chapter in this book. I repeat that advice for two reasons. First, to impress upon you how important those points are, and second, because this process really is that simple. I didn't say it was *easy*—but it is simple.

Whether or not you are comfortable with future transactions, and especially if you are not, you now have experience to share the lessons you have learned. Do your part to create the future leaders you would like to see in the world. This is what I will cover next. Now that you have acquired the treasures of the sea, it is time to share some of the bounty.

CHAPTER 9

A RISING TIDE LIFTS ALL BOATS

Congratulations! You are sailing smoothly and right on course to reach your destination. But can you really claim you did it by yourself? I am willing to bet your answer is no. You had support from investors, advisors, and mentors. Now it is your turn to support other sailors and would-be Captains. Here are a few examples to consider for how and why I personally find joy. Just as they do when finding a right-fit partner, people give back in different ways. As you think about ways to give back, align with your passion and what inspires you—just as you did when you founded your business. We all give back in different ways.

After every Royall & Company transaction, Bill encouraged everyone on his management team to take a portion of what we had made on the sale and invest it into a young founder in Richmond. That is how strongly he believed in paying it forward, and his legacy continues to. We were not even finished celebrating a transaction before he would remind us it was our commission to pick somebody we believed in and give them a chance. I had a spirit of giving before I met Bill. His devotion to philanthropy is one of the many reasons he will always inspire me.

Giving back is important for altruistic reasons but doing so is also beneficial in other ways. Have you considered that when you support up-and-coming founders, you also have a say in the future of businesses and business practices? Anyone can have an opinion on what they want to see in future leaders. At times founders may find themselves with too many voices and opinions pulling them in different directions. That can prove itself to be a distraction for a founder, slowing them down rather than allowing them to flourish in their growth. I encourage founders to ask advisors to demonstrate their belief by investing in founders.

Yes, I am recommending that you invest; as in to demonstrate through the investment of finances, time, and talents, your belief in the future growth and success of the founder and the business. Share your lessons learned in the industry or discipline where you have the personal experience a founder is seeking. It is important that giving-back initiatives are long-term oriented and not photo opportunities. It is better to demonstrate your commitment through your actions rather than simply stating a belief. Live your values in action and others will know your beliefs.

There are many ways to invest in the lives of founders.

In fact, this book is one of the ways I am investing in the lives of founders, by sharing my experience. Although I hope your journey inspires you to put "pen to paper" and write your own book to share your experiences with others, you do not necessarily have to go to all that effort. Maybe you have an interest in lecturing, mentoring, or serving on an advisory board of an organization you are passionate about. No matter where you are in your journey as a founder, you have gifts, talents, and experience to share with others. Do not fall into the trap of self-doubt that you do not have enough experience or wealth to become involved. Finding a way to give back starts early. Advisory boards need members with fresh perspectives, and especially those who are passionate about the mission of the organization. Start your commitment to serving others early. There are many ways to be an ally to entrepreneurs.

One of the things I enjoy is hosting the *Intimate Conversation Series* at MacLaurin Group, where we cover relevant topics best suited for smaller gatherings. Some are dedicated specifically to entrepreneurs. I invite private equity firms to talk to founders without any expectations on either side. Maybe the founder is not ready for private equity right now, but it is off in the horizon. I host conversations to support founders in their preparation—to get ready for when the timing is right. Entrepreneurs can ask questions, gain valuable information, and seek feedback without the pressure of pitching themselves. Sometimes the most valuable answer to your questions is not in response to a question you ask. It may be in the candor of an answer you hear in reply to someone else's brave vulnerability.

The goal of this is to bring people together whose orbits would never naturally intersect, in order to understand the path ahead and to demystify the challenges ahead.

Think of everyone you have ever admired. Not one of them did it alone. Think of all you achieved. You did not do it alone. Having the right mentor can inspire a young founder to hold onto the dream and make a positive change in the world. Who was your person who made you go left instead of right, look up instead of down? A good mentor will always open your eyes to your own possibility.

I met Roger Schnorbus, one of my mentors, in the MBA program at University of Richmond while taking his Strategic Management course. This course was brilliant. I decided to devote my free elective course requirement to take Strategic Mergers & Acquisitions, because Schnorbus also taught that particular course. Turns out that class would prove to be the hardest and most rewarding course of the entire program for me. As a retiree of the Campbell Soup Company where he held senior level positions including Director of International Product Development, Vice President of Corporate Product Development, and President of Mrs. Paul's Kitchens, Schnorbus had extensive firsthand experience.

What inspired me most about his Strategic Mergers & Acquisitions class was gaining the knowledge and experience of the idea that "there is no right answer, only right for you." Success in his course came down to your own research, valuation, alignment, and acceptance of risk. Ultimately you were expected to defend and persuade. For those willing to dig in, each case placed the student in the role of founder, CEO, investor, or private equity firm to find the right fit. Schnorbus was willing to spend countless office hours with me (and often with my two young children in tow) to debate assumptions and strategies of an acquisition target. He brought in industry experts to share their stories (often while the company was in the middle of a transaction process), to give our class an insider view. Of course, we were not privy to all the details of a transaction. Schnorbus would bring back our speakers later in the semester on the other side of a transaction to continue the fascinating stories we had read in the headlines. These lessons were timely, relevant, real world experiences that were most often kept behind closed conference room doors.

Schnorbus shaped my view of private equity leadership and the powerful role mergers & acquisitions have in growth strategies for businesses. In the years that followed, I continued to be a guest lecturer in his class, sharing my personal experience with mergers & acquisitions for others to debate. For me, it was an opportunity to recruit potential new hires with a passion for the industry.

If you are interested in being a guest lecturer or adjunct faculty, reach out to universities, talk to them about programs they have coming up in the next year, and let them know you have an interest. That way, they can be thinking about how best to use you in the curriculum in advance. And if you are currently a student, and feel inspired by a guest lecturer you hear, introduce yourself! Do not wait and try to get in touch with them later. Do not let them leave that room before approaching them. They showed up to be there for you because they are committed to the ecosystem.

When you mentor, you contribute to the success of future

leaders, and you might just unexpectedly meet a right-fit partner. In fact, Paymerang's Nasser Chanda and I met many years earlier, before he became a client of MacLaurin Group, through Schnorbus as we both agreed to be guest lecturers for him.

"Typically, people are either competitive or humble," says Chanda. "True leaders are both. Think about being competitive, happy, never satisfied, warm, service-minded, and also the sort of person who gives credit while taking blame. It is hard! Now also try to train others to be that way in order to embed true leadership deep into our culture."

You will not be surprised to hear that Chanda has put in place in his company an emerging-leaders program to invest in the next level of management.

THE MOST VALUABLE MOMENTS

"Paying it forward" might be as simple as participating in a heartfelt conversation. Being a good mentor does not mean you have all the answers and now you are willing to teach them to someone else. Young founders and entrepreneurs have skills and experience to bring to the table. I do not think of mentoring as just telling founders how to run their business. I think of mentoring as learning from each other.

As a case study, I will use Trilogy Mentors. In my research around Richmond, I kept hearing that this guy named John Failla was making an impact in education. Remember in chapter 1 when I told you about having coffee with a young founder whose story blew me away? That was Failla.

Growing up, Failla was (by his own admission) "a great lacrosse player and a horrible math student." Starting in fifth grade, his mom hired tutors for him but they never really worked because it was always more of the same. He was told he was not a good student. In seventh grade, his mom had enough and drove to the local high school to ask for the top math student.

Turns out that top math student, Josh, also happened to be an athlete, and was captain of a varsity team. The day Josh sat down to work with Failla on math, his entire perspective on education changed. Josh served as more than a tutor and became a mentor and role model to Failla. Josh took an interest in Failla and helped him not only in math, but also with the executive function of time management, setting weekly goals, and sitting down with Failla's mom after every lesson to give feedback on what had been covered.

It was the first time Failla had experienced the concept of relationship-based holistic learning. In the seventh grade, Failla saw a gap, or a customer pain point. In his senior year of college, he decided to start a business to address the roadblock of geographic location preventing students from being matched up with their best possible mentor.

This was a business about relationships. I realized the authenticity of Failla's drive; it was very personal and meaningful. He also shared his dedication to making the right choices for his clients, hiring and paying talented employees, and investing back into the business. The one thing keeping him up at night was technology. Our alignment was obvious. I wanted to do more than give him technology advice. I asked Bill Royall to sit down with the two of us, so Failla could sit across the table and learn from Bill. Even though Failla was in the middle of a round of fundraising, he did not ask Bill for a dime. He recognized that anyone could write him a check, but not anyone would have the advice and insight of a Bill Royall. Failla did not want to waste any of his time on a pitch. He was there to listen.

He asked how Bill had grown his business. He listened to the stories and wisdom of experience. Bill asked questions. Failla explained his growth strategy. Bill had a curiosity in this young man and gave him the gift of honest feedback. It was a respectful conversation comprised of challenging each other's thinking and perspectives; a meaningful engagement with no hubris. I watched as they learned lessons from each other.

I am especially eager to amplify the voices of people who want to make the world a better place, those founders with a noble mission. I tend to gravitate to founders who have plans to make other people's lives better. We all are our better selves when surrounded by those who believe in us.

Often, emerging founders exhibit new ways of thinking and solving problems. Working with them encourages you to weave new perspectives into your daily life. They can lead you to reshape your own lens. Supporting them benefits you.

The da Vinci Center at Virginia Commonwealth University is a collaboration of the University's Schools of the Arts and Business and the Colleges of Engineering and Humanities and Sciences. Its cross-disciplinary collaboration makes it a unique collegiate model for advancing innovation and entrepreneurship. As a result, says the center's executive director, Garret Westlake, "Students are better prepared to engage in our increasingly global world because they have developed the skills and tools necessary to engage in difficult dialog, to disagree, to reframe failure, and make change."

When I first met Westlake, it was clear he chose da Vinci because he wanted to be an active member of a community, and both Richmond and VCU have a strong commitment to community. You must apply to be a mentor with da Vinci and accept that you might not be accepted. "Great ideas and great leaders don't just come from talented, lucky people. They come from ecosystems that prioritize mentorship, collaboration, and a pay-it-forward mentality," says Westlake. He believes students and young founders need more than job opportunities and funding. They need mentors willing to invest in others before their own personal or corporate gain.

The center pairs mentors with students to ensure that every student accepted in the program will receive advice specific to their needs. Students must prove why they need money and what they are going to do with it, as well as pitch their ideas. Mentors are expected to give constructive feedback, the kind that allows students to fail and try again until they get it right. In the same way that I am passionate about connecting founders with right-fit partners, da Vinci is dedicated to matching students with mentors who can provide not only financial support, but also ideas and networking. It is truly a team environment.

In so much of education, students work on their own, test on their own, and get grades on their own. But where in business is anyone not leveraging collaboration? We are better together. In this kind of environment, students also learn how to foster the emotional intelligence required to work in teams and to communicate their ideas with one another. They learn how real companies work.

Then they literally go off and start real companies—sometimes working for each other. For those who chose not to start a business after graduation, we will see where their entrepreneurial spirit takes them in another three, five, or ten years. This is about the long game, increasing diversity and inclusivity in entrepreneurial and technical ecosystems.

As chairwoman for the Virginia Commonwealth University da Vinci Center for Innovation Angels Advisory Board, I have witnessed the evolution of Richmond as an innovation hub with a full complement of founders, investors, and programs alongside da Vinci, including Lighthouse Labs RVA, Health Innovation Consortium (VCU), Center for Innovation and Entrepreneurship (University of Richmond), Startup Virginia and Activation Capital. The Richmond ecosystem is positioned for future growth. In the words of Chandra Briggman, President and CEO of Activation Capital:

"Along my journey, I realized that if I were an entrepreneur, I could create one solution to one of society's problems. However, if I helped to build a larger pipeline of entrepreneurs, I could make a significantly larger impact solving more of the world's problems."

TEACH THEM MORE THAN HOW TO WIN

While mentoring, investing, and participating in emerging-leader programs, remember that one of the most positive impacts you can make for a founder is giving them a glimpse not only of what made you successful but also of times you failed. When a young founder hears about those, they get an invaluable perspective. They understand that even someone with lots of experience can make embarrassing and expensive mistakes.

They also get to hear how you got through it, how you pushed on and turned something really bad into something good. We read stories all the time about entrepreneurs who have made it. Chances are they also had moments when they were not successful. Stories of the latter can encourage founders not to give up.

When John Failla, Bill, and I had our conversation over coffee, I heard stories told that I had heard many times over the years and I reminisced on those while writing my book. Some have resonated more than others during the last twelve months, sometimes hitting closer to home than I would like to admit. As we came to the end of the conversation, Bill asked Failla if he had anymore questions, to which Failla asked what advice Bill would give to his younger self. Bill shared an honest account of how being an entrepreneur and a founder can absolutely absorb you if you let it. "Surround yourself with good people. Spend more time with those you love, friends, and family. Make more time for fishing trips."

This was before Bill discovered he had ALS. In fact, it was just before. He left the café inside the VCU Institute for

Contemporary Art to visit with his doctor that afternoon. First, there was still time for a brief tour of ICA, during which he shared stories of the passion he and his wife, Dr. Pam Kiecker Royall, share for art and philanthropy.

GIVE FOR YOURSELF

You can take what you have learned in business and apply those talents to almost any cause. Find your passion to give back to your community.

As chairperson on the board for Alzheimer's Association of Greater Richmond, I hope to amplify the voices of the thousands of volunteers and staff who dedicate their time to creating positive change in the lives of people and caregivers affected by this terrible disease. Our vision: A world without Alzheimer's and all other forms of dementia. I serve alongside mission-driven volunteers and leaders who inspire me. To share more about the organization with those you know impacted by the disease, please visit: alz.org/grva.

People often ask how I have the time to mentor, work with the da Vinci Center, guest lecture, work with the Alzheimer's Association, and build a business. The answer is that it all brings me joy. The people and the connections fuel me. Every time I walk away inspired, having learned something new—usually from someone who makes my running look like I am standing still. It is not exhausting. It is an honor, a blessing, and a gift. In that way, when you invest in others, you truly do invest in yourself.

If you need yet another reason to give of your time and

talents, I would remind you that when you give, you also demonstrate who you are and what you value in such a way that whenever you are later looking for a partner, it will be easier for that partner to recognize a right fit in you.

CONCLUSION

You may buy in to some of what I have written, all of it, or none of it. That is OK. That means you are doing exactly what I want you to do: figuring out what is the right fit for you. Only you know that. This book was delivered through my eyes in my experience. With this book, I hope I have given you the tools to find a partner who wants what is best for your business and has the specific expertise and resources to support you in achieving it. When you decide what is next for your business, I have full faith you will make the right decision, because the business would not exist without you.

Often, people think private equity partnership is only what I covered in chapters 6 and 7. Hopefully, the amount of ink I spilled on the preceding steps has left an impression on you. Egoless self-investigation is perhaps the most important step.

We have all heard that adage about relationships: "You can only love others as much as you love yourself." Growing your business with private equity is a relationship. You can only be as honest with others as you are with yourself. You can only trust others as much as you trust yourself. You can only recognize a right-fit partner when you recognize the lines and curves of your own fit.

If you have not done what you need to be that right partner, you absolutely will not find the private equity firm that will best support you as you grow your business. You might not find one at all.

For those who put in the work, though, there is a right-fit partner out there. And when you find them, you will be able to grow your business in ways you could not possibly have done without them. If you want to have that wonderful experience, you must position yourself to be their right partner on the other side of the table.

Preparing yourself for that started years ago. It started when you had a boss who led by example or a mentor you wanted to emulate. And it continued when you put into action the kind of founder you want to be. What I had in Bill was a leader who not only allowed me to be my authentic self, but who expected it of me, without question. He allowed me to have the responsibility and accountability to be fully vested, to know that I was making an impact. That is how I learned who I was as a leader and who I wanted to be "once again around the Cape."

PUT YOURSELF TO THE TEST

I have been fortunate to lead. And I have witnessed firsthand, from across the table, those moments and choices when a leader's integrity is put to the test. It is easy to say,

"I would definitely choose what is best for my clients and employees." It is a lot harder to deliver. You might know who you are on your best day. But do you know who you are on your worst day? And do you know how to make the kinds of decisions that can change what could have been the worst day into a best day?

Practice will turn these principles—being transparent with employees, checking in with customers in a way that is valuable to them, all of the things I call "Bill-isms"—into habit, and only then are you ready to really grow. The process of seeking investment comes on hard and fast. You will be pulled in many directions and face a seemingly endless series of choices, all of which need to be made now. There will be opportunities to take shortcuts, and you might think "just this once." Pause. Breathe. Hold true to your values.

Every choice you make becomes your legacy, becomes your path, and the path of all of your employees and clients. That is heavy. I know. It is yours as a leader to bear. Before seeking private equity, you need to know not only what your business needs and what you want in a partner, but you also must know what you are made of. Your daily work is not just sales, meetings, and development. It is also to be thoughtful and deliberate about who you are as a leader. Only after being tested will you be prepared to turn what could be a worst day into a best day.

SAILING IN A THUNDERSTORM

The dangers of sailing in a thunderstorm are obvious. No one willingly does so. Yet people get caught on the water unaware all the time. I remember hearing the pastor of my church give a sermon one Sunday morning about swimming in a thunderstorm. It struck me as a perfect metaphor for this process. When you as a founder find yourself sailing in a thunderstorm, there was a moment leading up to the storm when skies were clear and the water was smooth. And then, suddenly, you are stuck. Good sailors are defined by the rough seas not the smooth. And founders are often defined by how they respond to crises.

When it comes to partnering with private equity, crises can come in a few packages. The most common is a recession. Justin Marquardt is a principal at New Harbor Capital, who has participated in my Intimate Conversations series and who repeatedly demonstrates his commitment to supporting young founders. I asked what advice he would give young founders who are seeking private equity investment when the market hits a downturn.

"I would encourage them not to let market tumult distract from their focus on growth," he says. "A recession can naturally cause business leaders to think defensively. That definitely has its place, and in some instances is the only option, but it's important not to lose sight of the bigger picture, which is to continue to innovate and plan for growth. We [at New Harbor Capital] are growth investors, and wouldn't partner with a group if we didn't see growth potential."

Even if you were to receive a lower valuation than what you hoped for because of a recession, remember that it does not necessarily matter where you start because it is about where you are going. If you align yourself with someone who is focused on growth, then, well, they are focused on growth. And what better type of partner would you want than someone who is willing to take a chance, even during an economic downturn, because they see growth potential?

That does not mean weathering the storm will be easy. Have you ever been out on the water when a storm comes up quickly and unexpectedly? It is brutal. As you increase your speed to get to safety, every single small raindrop hits your skin like a thrown pebble or even a bee sting. If you tend toward seasickness, the rocking of the boat will quickly induce nausea. And any gear you did not tie down will either be damaged or become lost treasures at sea.

Riding out a thunderstorm on the open water is dangerous. It can even be fatal. You and your business may face challenges far more dangerous than a recession. People are flawed. People will disappoint you. People will disappoint themselves. Maybe even you as a leader will let yourself down.

People who know me as an exhausting ray of sunshine may be surprised to hear me say this, but having the courage to lose sight of the shore means you must accept the possibility of finding yourself treading water and fighting for survival. In those moments, stay true to your value system. Only you can decide how best to weather the storm. Some sailors will find shelter. Others will have to survive the bee stings until they stop.

IT IS TIME FOR YOU TO TAKE THE WHEEL

At the MacLaurin Group, we specialize in demystifying—in making things clear for our clients, whether private equity firms or founders looking for investment—so they are empowered to make strategic, beneficial decisions. That is what I have aimed to do with this book: demystify private equity partnership. My hope is that I have left you feeling comfortable with, prepared for, and excited about this harrowing but ultimately fulfilling process. If there is something that has resonated with you, I want to hear about it. If you think there is more to the story, let me know. You can contact me directly at Kelley@KelleyWPowell. com, find updates about my book at KelleyWPowell.com/, and learn more about MacLaurin Group at MacLaurin. Group.

I can also tell you what I do not want. I do not want for anyone to read this, think, *That is a great book,* and then do nothing with it. If you had a moment while reading this book when you thought, "I wish I had known that, I would have done something different," then do something different now. That is how you get ready to have what Bill and I call "circle-the-calendar-in-red days."

I guarantee there will be moments in your journey where, if you have the right mentors and leaders, and you know what you want and who you want to be, you will have those days. Because you will be prepared to act on game-changing moments, the kind you will look back on—whether it is securing one of your first clients, recruiting a superstar partner, or getting investment from your right-fit firm—and think, *That was the moment that changed everything.* You will circle that day in red.

Those moments are not the result of luck or talent. They happen when you have put in the work. Do not just put together a plan of when you are going to institute changes to be attractive to private equity. Institute them now.

Private equity partnership does not happen the moment you get a check or even months prior when you start developing your pitch. It started the moment you had a harebrained idea about a niche that needed filling. Part of why you became a founder is to control your own destiny. Private equity partnership does not negate that. It is an extension of it.

You are the one behind the wheel. You always have been. Of course you have the courage to lose sight of shore! If you did not, you never would have boarded the boat.

What now? Go find your partner, and set sail.

ACKNOWLEDGMENTS

To my family for the love, faith, support, and feedback. To my two young men most of all. Forgive me for the times I didn't always get it right. What I am most proud of in the world is being your mom.

To my business partners, Alan Williamson and Jim Headley, who stayed in the boat with me, both thinking it would be two days or at most two weeks—and now it has been over a decade. Thank you for your collaboration, support, and candor.

To the entire team at MacLaurin Group for building something really special.

To every client who has, and continues to, extend me the honor of their trust.

To Bill Royall for giving me the gifts of experiencing the story firsthand and sharing his lessons.

To Jane Borden for a list truly so long it needs semicolons

and dashes. Thank you for all the moments you took the wheel, especially when I needed rest.

To the entire team at Scribe: JeVon McCormick, Rikki Jump, Donnie McLohon, Kacy Wren, Jenny Shipley, Michael Nagin, Cristina Ricci, Rachael Brandenburg, Ian Claudius, and Zach Obront. Thank you for your guidance, creativity, dedication, and patience.

To Adam Coffey for the generous advice, genuine support, and enthusiasm.

To the private equity firms I call colleagues, clients, and friends who consistently prove there are really good people in this business.

To Garett Westlake and the entire team at da Vinci for truly investing in the lives of founders and our community.

To everyone who gave me the gift of their interview for this book. Thank you for sharing unique perspectives and allowing me to capture your voices.

To Dr. Pam Kiecker Royall and Kelley Stanley for your love and light.

To Roger Schnorbus for the inspiration and mentorship.

To each Royall & Company employee and every member of the senior leadership team who made us "and Company" (on good days and bad). It was only a story because each of us showed up.

To Cameron Herold for holding me accountable and introducing me to the amazing team at Scribe.

To Jani Parker for her gift of feedback, her sailor skills, and being one of the kindest humans on the planet. I'll set sail with you any day.

ABOUT THE AUTHOR

Kelley is CEO and Partner of MacLaurin Group, which she co-founded to provide technology operating partner services to high-growth organizations, portfolios of private equity companies, and investment groups. As a senior executive supporting the evolution of founder-led organizations through multiple private equity-led M&A cycles, Kelley's professional background includes more than twenty years of business building for high-growth companies.

Kelley is most sought after for her commitment to client success and value creation. As an avid mentor and angel investor, Kelley has a passion for building future entrepreneurs. She is a board member for ACG Richmond: Association for Corporate Growth, and a member of Virginia Council of CEOs. Kelley is the chairwoman of the da Vinci Center for Innovation Angels Advisory Board at Virginia Commonwealth University, guest lecturer at University of Richmond, and is currently a doctoral student at St. Thomas University in Leadership and Innovation with an emphasis on global business.

Kelley is passionate about her work as the chairperson for the board of the Greater Richmond chapter of the Alzheimer's Association, joining in the fight against this debilitating disease so that no one's memories are completely forgotten. Among all her endeavors and motivations, Kelley is inspired most in life by her two sons who have been her biggest cheerleaders throughout the years as she has balanced her roles in family and career.